ENDORSEMENTS FOR
"A NATIVE AMERICAN'S MESSAGE FOR AMERICA"
BY DON JOHNSON

Rev. Dr. Don Johnson's latest book, *A Native American's Message for America* is a message delivered from an unusual and unique perspective: The author's formative years of growing up as a member of the Makah Tribe. He brings a distinctive perspective to the complex issues facing all Americans, if not all human beings. Don's message is his response to these vital issues, clearly stated from his perspective as a Christian leader and Native American. His firm commitment to Biblical truth coupled with his unique background will afford his readers a new and useful vantage point in understanding our world today.

—Dr. William Heinicke, retired professor
Concordia University, Seward, Nebraska

I've known Rev. Dr. Don Johnson for many years and have found him to be an exceptional writer and storyteller. Rev. Johnson has a remarkable perspective that offers critical thinking to the events of our day. Having lived on an Indian reservation gave the author a first-hand view of socialism and its ruinous effects on the people it controlled. This book is extremely timely as we see events unfolding that demand our attention. His book easily engages the reader in its interesting discussion of world events and pivots the reader toward its significant implications. His insights and understanding are well thought out and consistent with what he knows is absolute truth.

—Pastor Richard A. Gordon
Brandon, South Dakota

As a Native American, and as a former chairman of the Makah tribal council, the Rev. Dr. Don Johnson offers his readers a unique and penetrating perspective of the fundamental issues that have been relentlessly chiseling away at the moral and political foundations of our society. An extremely insightful analysis of what has set our nation culturally adrift, and where we can find the only compass that will correct our course and restore sanity to our deeply troubled world.

—Rev. Ronald Hues, retired LCMS pastor

A NATIVE AMERICAN'S MESSAGE FOR AMERICA

REV. DR. DON JOHNSON

WESTBOW
PRESS®
A DIVISION OF THOMAS NELSON
& ZONDERVAN

WestBow Press books may be ordered through booksellers or by contacting:

WestBow Press
A Division of Thomas Nelson & Zondervan
1663 Liberty Drive
Bloomington, IN 47403
www.westbowpress.com
844-714-3454

All Scripture quotations are taken from the Holy Bible, NEW INTERNATIONAL VERSION®, NIV® Copyright © 1973, 1978, 1984, 2011 by Biblica, Inc.® Used by permission. All rights reserved worldwide

ISBN: 979-8-3850-2485-8 (sc)
ISBN: 979-8-3850-2486-5 (hc)
ISBN: 979-8-3850-2484-1 (e)

Library of Congress Control Number: 2024908781

Print information available on the last page.

WestBow Press rev. date: 06/12/2024

Contents

Preface

My Indian name is Owiktos. Derived from the Wakashan linguistic tradition and related to a small Native population on Vancouver Island, I cannot say for sure what the name means. Only that it once belonged to a distant ancestor and was passed down to me in the Native tradition at a name-giving ceremony by Isabel Ides, a valued elder and a part of my family tribal heritage.

I was encouraged to wear the name well by living an honest and good life to honor the memory of my deceased relative. It is in honor of him, my wife, Mary, who helped me immensely, my family heritage, and especially the Lord Jesus Christ, who at a crucial time in my life called me to faith and commissioned me to serve him in ministry, that I dedicate this book.

For reasons I cannot explain, it seems I was destined to write this book, even before I knew what to write or who Jesus was. The unique geography of my tribe at the end of America, our rich historical and cultural traditions, and my faith in God have afforded me a perspective on America I feel compelled to share.

This book is intended to be my message for America, one of warning and one of hope at a time when our country is currently going through incredible stresses and threats originating from the world of nature and politics. It is also intended as a wakeup call for Americans to reject the siren call of the Marxists who seek to turn America into a godless socialist state that can only lead to the destruction of freedoms and the end of the America we have known.

But even more importantly, it is a call for Americans to renew their reverence for our Creator God and to determine to honor His righteous laws. In doing so, He will bless our nation once again; America will be preserved.

Proverbs 14:3 affirms, "Righteousness exalts a nation, but sin condemns any people." And 2 Chronicles 7:14 says, "If my people, who are called by my name, will humble themselves and pray and seek my face and turn from their wicked ways, then I will hear from heaven, and I will forgive their sin and will heal their land."

Rev. Dr. Don Johnson

1

America at Land's End

This is what the Lord says, he who made the earth,
the Lord who formed it and established it—the Lord
is his name: "Call to me and I will answer you and tell
you great and unsearchable things you do not know."
—Jeremiah 33:2-3

WITH DAWN'S EARLY LIGHT CASTING BRILLIANT HUES OF SILVER
and gold just over the mountains of Washington State's Olympic
Peninsula, a remote region at the far end of the land gradually
awakens to welcome another day. My ancestors called this wondrous
place Quidicaa't ("the place where the birds gather at the end of the
land").

Surrounded on three sides by a vast ocean, this northwesternmost
edge of America is the land of my people, the Makah, who according
to archaeologists have resided in the area for well over three thousand
years.

Their name Makah conveys generosity and hospitality, as in
providing more than enough food and gifts for guests, especially
during their potlatch, or giveaway, ceremonies that remain an
important part of their cultural tradition just as in ancient times.
Blessed with an abundance of natural food resources—deer, elk, wild
berries, potatoes, clams, crabs, salmon, and halibut—and surrounded
by some of the most picturesque forests, mountains, and seas in

America, this land of abundance and beautiful scenery is where ancient tribal legend says humans were first created.

An artifact uncovered by archaeologists at the world-famous site of an ancient Makah village known as Ozette, an open clamshell with a carving of a little man lying inside it, brought to the memory of tribal elders an ancient creation narrative. According to the story, the first person created in the world was a woman who lived all alone in the land. Along with the beauty surrounding her, the Great Spirit had provided her with everything her heart could desire—gorgeous flowers and trees, a variety of bird and animal life, gentle hills and mountains, and expansive seas along with wonderful weather. But none of these were sufficient to console her frequent bouts with loneliness.

Day after day she would walk alone along beautiful stretches of white-sand beaches accompanied by the excited cries of gulls soaring high above in the gentle breezes. Yet for all the beauty of the land and sea and all the wondrous kinds of animals and birds the Creator had provided, the woman felt isolated, alone, and very sad.

In her moments of quiet desperation, she would plead with the Creator to provide a companion with whom she could share the joys of the land and seas along with all her hopes and dreams. But the Creator seemed oblivious to her desperate pleas.

But then one day while walking once more along the same lonely stretch of beach, a tear born of her sadness inadvertently fell onto a clamshell lying open-faced on the beach. Once the tiny teardrop splashed into the clamshell, it miraculously transformed into a little man who then was made by the Creator to mature into adulthood. You can imagine the woman's delightful surprise. Here finally was a helpmeet, someone like her. No longer alone, she now had a companion and friend, someone who would walk alongside her and with whom she could share the joys of life and fulfill the Great Spirit's intent to have male and female bring forth children who would eventually populate the entire earth.

It does seem a fanciful story to be sure, and I have embellished the background narrative with scenes I imagine would have been characteristic of such a beautiful place. Especially meaningful in the narrative passed down by the elders of my tribe was the characterization of the loneliness of the woman; it resembles the biblical story of Adam and Eve in that it has similar themes—most notably the creation of a helpmeet to complete and fulfill what had been missing. Adam was made to experience a deep sleep and Eve was formed out of his side. He was so pleased with Eve that he proclaimed, "This is now bone of my bones and flesh of my flesh; she shall be called 'woman,' for she was taken out of man" (Genesis 2:23).

Their unique bond forged from having been miraculously created—Adam from the dust of Mother Earth and Eve from his side—forms the basis for the sacred relationship of a man and a woman, leading to marriage and the beginning of families. And ever since, we—the distant family of Adam and Eve—have traced our ancestry to this great miracle. And like them, we too enter this world to be in a relationship first with God our Creator, then a man with a woman, and then Mother Earth.

2

The Unifying Principle

And forgive us our debts, as we also
have forgiven our debtors.
—Matthew 6:12

CERTAIN INSIGHTS ARE TO BE GAINED FROM THIS CREATION STORY
that is relevant for our present age, especially at a time when our
nation has been torn apart with increasing violence; divisiveness over
issues, such as the economy, the environment, gender issues, race,
past injustices, and whether reparations are owed; and disagreements
regarding the future of our form of government. None of this is
pleasing to God.

In His creative genius, our Creator made a diversity of people,
customs, cultures, and languages, and for that reason, different
though we may be, we share a common heritage as brothers and sisters
in the family of God; we are His children, and He would have us live
together in peace and harmony. And while we vary in appearance and
ethnicity, we are created in our Creator's image and equal in His eyes,
a truth affirmed by the Declaration of Independence.

> We hold these truths to be self-evident that all men
> are created equal, that they are endowed by their
> Creator with certain unalienable rights, that among
> these are Life, Liberty and the pursuit of Happiness.

This founding principle of the American Constitution, while

not always applied to its citizens equally, forms the basis for our constitutional freedoms and the right to shape our individual destinies without government intrusions. They are born out of America's Judeo-Christian heritage. What is especially unique in our country is that regardless of our ethnicity or individual circumstances, under the laws that govern our nation, any one of us can rise above our circumstances to become the best person our individual talents allow.

Unfortunately, there are those who would intentionally cause divisions among us by highlighting our differences and encouraging racial tensions by reminding people of past injustices and amplifying new ones, a strategy whose ultimate purpose is to create radical social change in America. In the world of politics, the current effort to divide by class and race is straight out of the playbook of the Marxist/socialist strategy of fomenting division among the masses to drive the social change they seek to attain. It is not to say we can or should ignore the consequences that result from our nation's past sins, especially those rising out of the formation of America when treatment of Native Americans was at its worst and slavery was introduced. And for that reason, we should, as a moral nation whose laws were rooted in biblical values, be especially sensitive to those of our citizens whose ancestors were subject to abuses and then do what a moral nation should to amend past unjust policies. In doing so, however, we should not create a culture of victims and perpetrators or create dependencies. Rather, programs to help people should encourage freedom, self-reliance, and independence.

The reason I can speak to this is that I was raised in a Native community whose people a generation or two before me were stripped of their right to determine their futures and deceived into signing away most of their traditional lands. In most instances, children were taken from parents and placed in faraway boarding schools whose purpose was to educate the Indian out of Native children. Native Americans were not granted citizenship until 1924. In the aftermath, alcoholism, poverty, loss of hope, and especially the debilitating impacts of the imposition of the reservation system, an early application of socialism in America, joined as one to inhibit self-determination and eradicate Native people's potentials. It resulted in dependency, not freedom, especially as government programs to help Indian tribes were created that further ensured this would occur. This was the origin of the Bureau of Indian Affairs and the reservation system.

This was big government at its worst: enlarged government controls and diminished freedom for those forced to endure it. Since this was the world I was exposed to from an early age, God had to teach me to see a broader vision of world history: that in a world beset by sin, tragedies and injustices of all sorts have always been a part of the human experience.

The Creator wanted me to understand that there is a context to the human experience. All people at some point in their unique histories have had ancestors who were victims of injustice or been the cause of the same. No race is exempted from sin. In Romans 3:23, the apostle Paul concluded, "For all have sinned and fall short of the glory of God."

There is but one cure for the human condition: the willingness to humbly acknowledge our sin, repent and ask Jesus's forgiveness, and allow His grace to work in our hearts in a way that empowers us to love and to forgive others. Forgiveness is at the heart of the gospel message, and regardless of our racial heritage, we are all sinners in need of God's forgiveness offered through Jesus.

Assigning blame and playing on past injustices by those intent on dividing America into the haves and have-nots, the privileged versus those who are not, couldn't be more antithetical to the gospel message. Why can I say this? Jesus, more than anyone in the history of the world, endured prejudice and injustices to the point of being crucified on the cross for our sins. God the Father poured out on Jesus His wrath for our sins. It was Jesus's willingness to take upon Himself our sins and experience the wrath of God we deserved that has afforded us the opportunity to experience the forgiveness of our sins. In Isaiah 53:4–5, we read,

> Surely, he took up our pain and bore our suffering, yet we considered him punished by God, stricken by him, and afflicted. But he was pierced for our transgressions, he was crushed for our iniquities; the punishment that brought us peace was on him, and by his wounds we are healed.

If we would be more like him in our relationships with one another, all our prejudices, hurts, and divisiveness would melt away, and our ancient wounds would be healed and our legacy as a great nation would be preserved. And we would begin to understand that we are called to live together in this time and place as brothers and sisters in Christ to achieve a greater purpose.

This became evident to me when I read the apostle Paul's remarkable sermon to a Greek audience in Athens, Greece, two thousand years ago. In his message to the learned scholars on Mars Hill, he declared, "From one man he made all the nations, that they should inhabit the whole earth; and he marked out their appointed times in history and the boundaries of their lands" (Acts 17:26).

It is clear from this that we live in America because God, according to His sovereign will, determined from eternity that America would one day be our homeland and for one all-important reason.

By raising up the American nation and placing us in this land in this time, no matter our ethnicity or the circumstances that got us here, we have a unique opportunity to receive and to experience the grace offered through His Son Jesus. And then, having received the gift Jesus offers, sharing that same message of hope with our fellow citizens.

In Acts 17:27 Paul explained the underlying intent of our Creator. "God did this so that they would seek Him and perhaps reach out for Him and find Him, though He is not far from any one of us."

What more unique place than America, the great melting pot of nations, and blessed with unprecedented freedom of religion and expression, to experience the salvation Jesus offers and of whom it is said, "And with your blood you purchased for God persons from every tribe and language and people and nation" (Revelation 5:9)? Therefore, regardless of the circumstances that brought our forefathers to this land, whether just or unjust, we are here because God determined from all eternity that America would be our homeland.

And in finding Him, experiencing His grace so that we in turn can offer that grace to our fellow citizens.

In recent years, this truth has been obfuscated by those who want to fundamentally change America into a godless socialist state.

I remember attending grade school when at the beginning of each day we would stand at attention while looking up at the American flag in front of the room and in unison, with my classmates, saying,

> I pledge allegiance to the flag of the United States
> of America and to the republic for which it stands,
> one nation under God, indivisible and with liberty
> and justice for all.

The Marxists'/socialists' efforts to divide us into the haves and have-nots, the privileged versus those who are not, are at their core a direct affront to our Christian heritage and the Gospel of God's grace. Its ultimate purpose is to undermine the purpose God intended for this nation.

America has been a great nation because God has blessed us, and Jesus is and has always been the Great Unifying Principle that binds us as one.

3

Lessons from Creation

In the beginning of all things, wisdom and
knowledge were with the animals, for Tirawa, the
One Above, did not speak directly to man. He sent
out certain animals to tell men that he showed
Himself through the beasts, and that from them,
and from the stars and the sun and the moon
should man learn that all things tell of Tirawa.
—Eagle chief, Pawnee, nineteenth century

PRIOR TO THE COMING OF THE EUROPEANS, THE LAND AT THE FAR
edge of America I described in chapter 1, not only afforded a wide
variety of food, its rugged terrain and gorgeous sand beaches inspired
a unique culture, one that reflected the unique bond my people forged
with the land and sea the Creator had made.

By carefully observing the behavior of birds and animals, the
cycle of the seasons and the winds and tides, my ancestors gradually
learned lessons they could pass on to succeeding generations in the
form of story, song, dance, and their arts.

Very often, tribal elders related to the children of the community
timeless stories of animals interacting with humans. Many of these
were humorous and always taught important life lessons about
diligence, hard work, and honesty.

So connected to the creature world were northwest coastal people
that it was believed that if someone walking in the forest heard an

owl call out his or her name, it meant their death or someone in their family was not far-off.

In my travels as head of a Christian ministry that served Alaska Natives, I recall an elder from a small, remote, Native community sharing the tragic story of five young men from their village who had recently gone fishing and lost their lives at sea. Their bodies were never recovered. But then an amazing occurrence: during a memorial service held in their honor, five killer whales appeared in the bay adjacent the community circling round and round as if to assure the grieving community all was well. As the orcas were circling, high above, a lone bald eagle flew in seeming concert with them. This surprised no one in the village.

One of the more well-known creatures northwest tribal lore was Raven, a legendary bird possessed of magical powers. One of the smartest of God's bird creation, Raven in northwest coast tribal tradition was often depicted as a trickster or jokester. He was not only able to communicate with humans but was always on the lookout to defraud the unwary or foolish.

Fortunate to have been born at a time when many of the traditional people were still around to tell my generation stories of animals interacting with people, my boyhood friends and I learned early on to respect Mother Nature and to appreciate that the creature world and nature itself could communicate lessons.

Learning to appreciate and respect the power of the vast ocean was of primary importance to the children of my community, especially since generations of our people had been so dependent on all that it had to offer.

One of my best childhood friends, a boy named Glenn, and I would typically roam the beaches in front of our community in search of flat-surfaced drift logs weathered but still very buoyant. These would serve our purposes as paddleboards do today.

It was great fun, and risky of course, to be paddling our makeshift paddleboards around the bay, especially since Glenn had not yet learned to swim and I was a novice myself. Nevertheless, it was activities like these that were not only great fun, but they also taught us not to fear the sea but rather to respect its many moods.

Naturally, had my mother known what we were doing, she surely would have been quite concerned. This although she knew Native children throughout the generations typically paddled small canoes in the shallows of the bay while emulating the whale hunt after the tradition of their forefathers. The hunt for whales by tribal men chosen for their skills had a long and storied history, which I will explain later.

Having tired of our adventures, my friend and I would build sandcastles buttressed with barriers of sand, rocks, seashells, or whatever else we could find to withstand the inevitable surge of the incoming tide.

Despite our best efforts, the relentless waves always overwhelmed our efforts. These beginning lessons, however futile, helped to reinforce the message we had been taught: nature is a formidable force that demanded respect.

Above the beach where much of our play activity occurred is the present town of Neah Bay, the last of the original five settlements of my people and the place where my message for America first began to take on substance.

Already as a youth I was beginning to see that things around me were changing, and it was occurring at a quickening pace. Not only were the older generation of my people gradually passing on, but my generation was beginning to experience a world vastly different from theirs.

4

Catalysts for Change

ONE OF THE MORE IMPACTFUL CATALYSTS FOR CHANGE IN MY SMALL corner of the world came as the result of the construction of a winding gravel road connecting our community with the outside world.

Before it was built, the only way in or out of our community was by boat. The gravel road, constructed along the Strait of Juan de Fuca, enabled people for the first time to traverse more readily to the nearest town with services, some seventy miles distant. This enabled another change agent, automobiles.

New opportunities for the locals to buy cars, find work, get an education, buy goods, see a doctor, and travel to far-off places were now made more possible. And one other less desirable change was people could now access alcohol much more easily.

During World War II, the Korean War, and the later Vietnam War, almost all the men in my community able to serve were drafted or volunteered to join the army. They were typically assigned to the front lines, where they faced significant combat in Europe and later in Korea and Vietnam.

If you are a veteran of the military, you know what it must have been like for some of these men upon returning home. For those suffering the effects of PTSD and having been exposed to alcohol during their time serving in the military, this would be a major problem once their military service ended, especially with the recently constructed road that made beer and whiskey more easily attainable.

Alcoholism soon became problematic. When I was a child, my father under the influence lost control of his truck while traveling the winding coastal road, resulting in the death of his passenger and serious injuries that would plague him throughout the rest of his life.

Then there was the danger associated with the large diesel log trucks that regularly traversed the gravel road, often spinning large clouds of swirling dust that obscured one's view.

Over the course of years, a few accidents occurred when those who attempted to get around the often-slow moving tractor trailers met oncoming vehicles. Today the road is much safer since it has been paved.

Despite the conditions, the road served as an accelerant for change as it encouraged innovation.

Sometime around the 1940s, a diesel-powered generator plant was built, enabling the community to have electricity for the first time.

Not long after, resorts and cafes and several motels were added to afford recreational users opportunity to fish salmon and halibut, which in those days were very abundant. Eventually, the town added several gas stations, a movie theater, indoor plumbing, and toward the end of the 1950s, rotary telephones and the first televisions.

Ironically, two of the tribe's leading elders, Harold and Isabelle Ides, born in the previous century and well acquainted with the old ways, were the first to purchase a black-and-white TV. Other tribal members did the same thing. Before long, antennas were sprouting up on rooftops throughout the village.

In the beginning, television reception was primitive, consisting of grainy, almost impossible to make out black-and-white images. The sound was often garbled. None of that mattered or the fact that we had only two usable channels: one originating out of Canada and the other out of Bellingham, Washington. We were fascinated by this innovation.

Our formerly isolated Native American community at the "end of the land where the birds gather" had been introduced to an entirely new way of life. My generation was caught between the world that was slowly fading into the background and a new one emerging.

5

Old Ways and New Ways

No one remembers the former generations,
and even those yet to come will not be
remembered by those who follow them.
—Ecclesiastes 1:11

EVEN WITH THE ENCROACHMENT OF EVERYDAY AMERICAN LIFE, there remained something about my community reminiscent of the ancient way of life.

Parked along the beach just below the modern businesses were traditional, hand-carved, cedar dugout canoes, relics from a distant era. Some were forty feet in length.

During the 1950s, when the Makah Tribe was just beginning to experience rapid change, forty-foot, hand-carved, cedar dugout canoes utilized for thousands of years to hunt whales or to fish for salmon and halibut were still being utilized.

Some of these canoes lined the beaches. And although whaling was no longer permitted by federal law, you might find an old harpoon or the remains of a sealskin float bag stored under someone's house. And some of the older men continued their canoe-building craft by acquiring large cedar trees from Vancouver Island, the place where the largest trees could be found, and then with adze and axe shaping what had once been a proud tree into a forty-foot, eight-man canoe. The process was more involved than what I describe here, but my point is simply to illustrate how the ancient traditions were still being practiced.

14

My father started his fishing career in one of these hand-carved canoes. He would typically paddle his canoe far out to sea using the outgoing tidal currents to hurry his canoe along to his preferred fishing area. In the tradition of the ancients, he was able to determine where to fish, often using nothing more than a landmark on the far shore or a distant rock formation arising out of the sea to align his canoe with the proper location.

Once on site, and with a traditional handline and halibut hook called a *chibu'ud*, often baited with herring or octopus, my father could pull a thousand pounds of halibut in a day. Then he would return with the in-rushing current to our village, where he would sell his catch for five cents per pound. The $50 he received in return was not bad for a day's work. Fishing out of canoes wasn't the only remnants of the past.

Born in the latter part of the nineteenth century, many of the elders in the 1940s and 1950s still spoke the Makah language. They seemed to me to be of a quiet demeanor, never too forward but always willing to listen and answer any questions. As a child in those earlier days, I regret not taking more time to listen to their wisdom.

I recall them to be great storytellers and experts on certain plants and natural herbs that served as cures for a variety of illnesses.

For that reason, preserving their knowledge was considered a priority and a vitally important contribution to the overall health of the tribe.

Unfortunately, with the passing of these valued members born of a distant world along with the government-imposed efforts to discourage Native traditions, much of the ancient wisdom of the elders has been lost. This was costly to our tribe and to the many other Native American communities throughout North America.

Sadly, one of the ironies I see unfolding in America today is something very similar to what Native peoples have had to endure.

The wisdom of this nation's elders, and by that I mean the founders of the American republic and contributors to the US Constitution, is increasingly coming under deliberate attack by Marxist-influenced progressives intent on discrediting their perspective on such important matters as freedom of speech and religion and other aspects of our individual rights.

I suspect some of the Native elders I knew as a child, were they alive today, would recognize how similar the efforts to discredit the legacy of America's founders resemble the government-imposed policies designed to discourage Native Americans from speaking their language or practicing their cultural traditions. These efforts along with the creation of the reservation system and the introduction of government controls greatly impacted the Native way of life. Many tribes still haven't recovered.

Social scientists have long recognized the challenges Native Americans have faced due to government policies that discouraged the old ways while introducing rapid change. They described it as "culture shock," meaning that too radical of change that obliterates the people's past values and traditional practices eventually overwhelms the individual's ability to adapt. This ultimately leads to nihilism, a condition whereby there are no longer tried and true values and beliefs to guide one's life.

The cost to Native American tribes has been enormous and includes poverty, high rates of suicide, drug addiction, spousal abuse, and loss of purpose. I will discuss more fully how nihilism, the absence of spiritual and moral guidelines, invites satanic influence.

My point here is to illustrate how nihilism is no longer descriptive of Indian tribes alone. Our entire country has begun to lose its way as it goes through rapid change and no longer acknowledges our Christian heritage as before.

Part of this is the result of the same forces for change that affected my people and some orchestrated by the Marxists who hijacked our educational institutions to further their godless philosophies. They are at their core anti-Christian and opposed to the basic presumptions of the Christian faith.

But more important than their diabolical efforts to undermine our nation's spiritual heritage is the willingness on the part of many of our citizens to go along with them by willingly forsaking faith in our Creator and the moral values that shaped this nation's founding principles. This is suicidal on a national level, and the result has been that we have lost the grace God gives His people to discern right from wrong or retain sanity in an insane world.

America, if it continues this trend away from God and its socialist path toward big government, will become one big reservation. Having experienced reservation life imposed by socialism, I can say with conviction, "America, you don't want this."

For now, I will relate how my worldview, especially as concerns America, began to be shaped out of the obscure world where I grew up and the changes that affected me, my family, and my tribe.

I continue my message for America with an unusual childhood adventure, finding treasure in my family's backyard.

6

Treasure in Our Backyard

I DID NOT COME TO MY VIEWS CONCERNING AMERICA WITHOUT first having been exposed to certain experiences living among my people that afforded me a unique perspective. These, along with an interest in world history, contributed to the formation of my message.

From the beginning of the colonial expansion period in the fifteenth and sixteenth centuries, the land of my people located at the far edge of what is now America was recognized by early explorers from various nations for its vast resources and its strategic importance.

Naturally, expeditions by Spain, Britain, France, Russia, Portugal, and the developing nation of America eventually resulted in disputes over land claims.

Among the first to arrive in my part of the world intent on exploiting its resources and claiming the land for their own nation were the Spanish. Beginning with Columbus, the Spanish influence spread rapidly throughout South America and North America including the present states of Florida, New Mexico, Arizona, Texas, California, Oregon and Washington state.

As early as 1592, Juan de Fuca, a Greek sailor employed by Spain, arrived in his sailing ship to explore the region where my people reside. His name was assigned to the body of water, the Strait of Juan de Fuca, that separates my community from Vancouver Island.

By 1792, the Spanish, as was their custom, officially staked claim to my people's land in the name of the Father, the Son, and the Holy Spirit and in the name of the king and queen of Spain.

Not long thereafter, they built a fort, naming their newest colony Nunez Gaona, after a famous Spanish naval admiral.

The small fort situated next to a creek on the west end of the small town of Neah Bay where I spent my childhood consisted of emplacements for five cannons, a building to prepare and store food, and a barracks with sufficient room for eighty men.

The Spanish didn't stay long, and the reason for this is suggested in the discovery of a treasure my older brother Leonard and I found while playing a childhood game in our backyard.

Setting sibling rivalry aside, my brother would occasionally invite me to accompany him on one of his insatiable quests for some new adventure of one sort or another.

Because there were times when I was the foil of some of his pranks, I looked forward to those opportunities when he would invite me, his little brother, to join him on another one of his adventures; these would always usher in the best of times.

Naturally living on the far edge of America in a kind of Huckleberry Finn and Tom Sawyer setting, great adventures real or imagined seemed always around the next bend in the river or, in our case, the next beach over.

One bright summer morning, my brother invited me to play outside. In our search for something to do, we noticed a rusty pickaxe leaning against the backside of our house.

What was going through our childish minds I cannot begin to explain, except that we decided to use the worn and rusted pickaxe to assault an imaginary enemy represented by a rotting stump on the edge of the forest near our home. The old stump had been there long before I was born, the remains no doubt of what a proud Sitka Spruce or Cedar tree had once been. Its very presence beckoned us to engage in battle.

With our imagined enemy fixed firmly in front of us, we took turns violently attacking the stump. As we made our courageous assault, bits and pieces of decayed wood began to fly in every direction.

I think we were winning the battle. But then amid our onslaught, we heard the distinctive sound of metal on metal as the pointed edge of our pickaxe struck something metallic buried deep within the heart of what remained of the ancient tree.

Ever vigilant in any of our adventures, Leonard's eyes grew wide with excitement. His voice betraying heightened anticipation, he turned to me and said, "Hey Donald! Did you hear that? Something is inside this stump!"

"Yeah," I responded. "I heard that too."

Because I looked up to my brother, I was always ready to embrace whatever he said. And his obvious excitement said this was big—I mean really big. We had just discovered buried treasure right in our own backyard!

Caught in the excitement of the moment, our imaginations running wild with expectation, we dug feverishly into the decayed remains to uncover our prize.

Although neither of us knew its significance, the pickaxe blade had struck something far more noteworthy than the gold or silver we believed might be hidden in the stump. We had uncovered an ancient but perfectly preserved cannonball.

What was it doing in the old stump? And for how long had it been there? It was a mystery.

Using our bare hands, we feverishly removed the remaining shards of rotted wood that held it captive. Finally freeing it from its prison, my brother proudly raised the baseball-size cannonball in his hands for me to examine.

We were disappointed though. It was little more than a curiosity. We took it home, and my mom put it on a mantel.

Eventually as I grew older and began to take an interest in world history, I realized that the cannonball represented an idea that was beginning to engulf the whole world of your ancestors and mine.

The New World, as it came to be known, was being readied for colonization by those in possession of superior technology; things like large seaworthy sailing ships, navigation instruments, cannons, and other weapons could be used to frighten and subdue the Natives.

The nations possessing technological advantages like cannons and cannonballs were European. Many of them were running out of resources in their homelands, and others, anxious to escape oppressive governments, were willing to leave their familiar land to find better opportunities in the New World.

The New World, rich in gold, silver, furs, vast forests, and foods of all kinds, was the ideal place to begin anew.

And even though the intent of the Creator was to have humankind disperse across the face of Mother Earth, He never willed enslavement, theft of land and resources, and all the evil deeds that accompanied the colonial expansion era.

His greater purposes, amid the darkness of a world caught up in greed and lust for power and dominance, are always intended for good and not evil.

And while the cannonball was a small relic, a symbol of the worst aspects of human interactions, it represented an era when the continents of Mother Earth were being readied for colonization by a diversity of people. And that was clearly a part of God's greater plan to have people multiply and disperse throughout the entire world.

7

A Global Worldview

My brother and I were in grade school when we discovered the cannonball. Little did I know at the time that it would eventually contribute to my interest in global affairs, especially how the American nation was formed.

In the meanwhile, the cannonball was little more than a curiosity. There it sat on a mantel in our living room until a few years later when, following a move from our reservation to the city of Tacoma, my younger brother decided to take it to his new primary school for show-and-tell.

In an unguarded moment, someone decided to steal it. Was it the teacher? Another student? My parents, perhaps because they were new to life off the reservation, were reluctant to go to the school and insist that it be returned.

It was disappointing of course that someone would take advantage of the situation and steal such a unique artifact.

Nevertheless, by the time the theft occurred, I had developed a burgeoning interest in world history, eventually figuring out that the cannonball had been fired at my people in anger during an era when European nations were expanding their territorial claims throughout the world.

The fort the Spanish had built was obviously an example of this. It was not long after it was constructed that serious conflict erupted, the result of an apparent incident between a Makah woman and a Spanish soldier.

In the end, the Spanish soldier was killed by some of the Makah men. This led to increased tensions, eventually resulting in the Spanish firing their cannons at a canoe in the bay in front of our village with women and children onboard.

Some of the passengers in the canoe were killed in the incident. Naturally, this heightened tensions even more, which explains why a cannonball was imbedded in the old stump behind our house.

A likely relic from this ancient conflict, the cannonball my brother and I uncovered apparently missed its intended target and instead embedded in a tree at the edge of the forest that would one day serve as my family's backyard.

As a way of mending the memory of this ancient conflict, to their credit, the government of Spain in recent years built a monument in honor of Makah war veterans in the very place where their fort once stood.

Although there are many remnants of ancient leftovers of war like the cannonball we found throughout the world, this one was especially meaningful to me because of where we found it and its connection to a critical era in our shared history, a time when the boundaries of nations were being defined and disputes among nations over their respective claims were being settled.

Since I was too young to make much of this at the time we made our discovery, I never gave its significance much thought until years later.

In my readings of history, I came across ancient occurrences that helped me to piece together our shared history, events set in motion long before we were born that eventually connected your fate with mine.

8

Aristotle and the Indians

FROM THE MID-FIFTEENTH CENTURY TO THE LATE 1700S, AS I previously related, nations like Spain, Portugal, Italy, Holland, Russia, France, England, and the soon-to-be established United States were fully engaged in sending explorers to far-off lands.

The intent was to survey, map, and evaluate resources and secure land claims for their respective countries regardless of any inherent claims by the original inhabitants.

Such were their successes that by the end of the nineteenth century, much of the earth's landmass was claimed by one European nation or other.

European nations during the Discovery Era had been influenced in their discovery efforts in large part by a revival of the ancient Greek and Roman classics, including the writings of none other than the famed Greek philosopher and founder of Western civilization, Aristotle.

His monumental treatise *The Politics*, written in 350 BC, dealt with the purpose of government, law, ethics, science, logic, and empirical research—all great contributions to the development of Western thought.

As enlightening as his influence was in respect to these disciplines, there were, however, fatal flaws in his thinking. Although an evident genius, his political view that humankind was made up of the "civilized" and what he called "barbarians," or uncivilized people, was to have profound impacts on the imposition of slavery and the treatment of Native Americans.

In his treatise, he stated that some people were natural-born lords and others were natural born slaves. "For that some should rule, and others be ruled is the thing not only necessary but expedient; from the hour of their birth, some are marked out for subjection, others for rule."[1]

This was not a new idea since prejudice toward others and slavery has existed among all people throughout human history, including my tribe. However, Aristotle's thought had a particularly important role in shaping European history at a critical time.

Describing a policy that would serve as a model for European nations during the Discovery Era, he declared civilized nations were justified in seizing the lands and resources of barbarians in exchange for civilizing them.

In practice, this usually meant subjugation and slavery, theft of resources, and almost no benefits for the conquered.

His ideas would have profound impacts nearly two thousand years later when the Discovery Era had begun, eventually providing justification for the theft of lands and natural resources wherever European colonization took place.

Naturally, this created a moral dilemma. How could the Christian nations of Europe justify their treatment of those they considered barbarians when Christian doctrine taught equality of the races and justice for all? This troubling dilemma was solved by a papal decree.

---

[1] Jowell, Benjamin. *A Translation of Aristotle's Book One, Politics*, Section V., 350 BC.

9

Romanus Pontifex

WHAT HISTORY ULTIMATELY REVEALS ABOUT HUMAN INTERACTIONS is that there is never an end to humankind's creative genius in justifying evil. This was true then as now.

To resolve the moral dilemma facing Christian nations during the Discovery Era, Pope Nicholas issued a papal bull or public decree in 1452, forty years before Columbus, that provided justification for European conquest of distant lands.

In his decree titled "Romanus Pontifex" issued to King Alfonso of Portugal, the pope afforded a "moral" guideline for European conquest. He declared that those countries with a Christian heritage, meaning European nations, had a moral right to claim lands from "pagans and enemies of Christ" and "to take all their possessions and property."

This synthetizing of Aristotelian thought with Christianity formed the basis for what came to be known as the Doctrine of Discovery.

Eventually the fifteenth-century papal decree linked to Aristotle's ideas slowly worked its way through succeeding centuries to American policy regarding Native Americans. This is illustrated by a ruling made in 1823 by the US Supreme Court.

Under Chief Justice John Marshall's leadership, the Supreme Court agreed to adopt a federal law declaring that the Doctrine of Discovery was applicable to the US government's treatment of Indians.

America after all had its roots in Europe and met the standard of being a Christian nation. Native Americans, on the other hand, were regarded as uncivilized pagans and enemies of Christ, undeserving of their lands.

Although it took years for the Supreme Court's ruling to finally impact my tribe living on the far end of the Olympic Peninsula, the inevitable consequences were never far-off.

Once the US government established ownership of the Pacific Northwest in the 1820s and 1840s following agreements first with Spain and later the British, the American government justified seizing tribal lands, restricting the speaking of their languages, and the subsequent removal of children from their homes and placing them in boarding schools based on the idea of civilizing the barbarians articulated by Aristotle.

Ironically, whether government policymakers in the nineteenth century understood it or not, this was the implementation of the three pillars of socialism: seize the occupants lands, destroy their economy, and take away the people's freedom to determine their own destinies. The Great White Father in Washington, DC, was now in charge.

Accompanying this early socialist experiment to force change was the introduction of something you might find surprising. It was the mechanical clock. Although the new way of marking time was resisted by tribes throughout the Americas, its invention was a driving force in the development of American industry. That however was not its original purpose.

For Europeans, the mechanical clock invented sometime in the fourteenth century by an obscure monk was designed to advance worship and coordinate prayer times. But like any innovation, it had other applications. It eventually enabled Europeans to break free from nature's seasonal cycles, especially the restraints imposed by the amount of daylight available during the year.

Key to the development of the clock was the invention of an "interrupter" or, as it is better known, an "escapement device." Connected to cogs, weights, ropes, and the bell calling people to worship, this innovation allowed the precise check and released interval or ticktock measurement of clock time.

So important an innovation was the mechanical clock that historian Daniel Boorstin concluded,

> There are fewer greater revolutions in human experience than the movement from the seasonal or "temporary" hour to the equal hour. Here was man's declaration of independence from the sun, new proof of his mastery over himself and his surroundings ... Sun time was translated into clock time.[2]

Europeans were now free to live and work in sync with the ticktock of the clock and not the amount of available daylight. Later innovations like the pendulum, springs, wheels, and gears enabled more accuracy, allowing for the segmenting of time into hours, minutes, and seconds. It was not long before Europeans could have clocks within their homes and even on their wrists.

These improvements in time management enabled Europeans to better coordinate industry, measure things more accurately, and improve navigation, which facilitated colonization during the discoverers' long voyages to the Americas and beyond.

Soon the design that went into the clock contributed to the development of the machinery of industry. The Industrial Revolution soon followed, and with it, a requirement for more natural world resources and laborers and mass production in less time.

For Europeans, time like money had become a commodity; it could be wasted, invested, or lost. And ever since, the world has been driven by the ticktock of the clock and the natural world has felt the brunt of its supremacy. And we in turn have felt the stress of not having enough time or enough resources. We often find ourselves "out of time," and we always need more and more resources to drive our economy.

A consequence of this is that the natural world has experienced much distress as there is always the demand for more and more

---

[2] Boorstin, Daniel. *The Discoverers*. New York: Random House, 1985.

resources. And the mental health of American families suffers stress from having to have two parents work to afford the means to purchase a home, a car or afford education opportunities for their children.

For traditional Native Americans, however, time was for nurture of tribe and family. The purpose of life was to live in harmony with the natural world's cycles, not to gain mastery over it.

Undaunted by the requirements of time-driven progress afforded my people and eventually me a more traditional view of Mother Nature. Living alongside the wondrous creation, we were on "Indian time," and that meant we had plenty of time for each other and time to learn to read creation's declarations.

This is not intended to be a criticism of the mechanical clock and all that it has meant to the development of this nation's industry. Rather, it is a recognition of two kinds of time that exist in the world. And a call for there to be a healthy balance between these two ways of marking time that preserves time for our relationships with our Creator (the original intent of clock time), with each other and the creation while also allowing for innovation that enhances life and does not destroy it.

The seasonal return of the salmon, so much a part of their diet, gave my people a unique insight into the cyclical design the Creator built into His creation.

10

The Cycle of Life

LONG BEFORE THE ARRIVAL OF OUR CLOCK-DRIVEN BROTHERS AND sisters from Europe and later people from other parts of the world, my people called their part of America Quidicaa't ("the place where the birds gather at the end of the land").

It was in this primeval place of wilderness, mountains, seas, forests, and lakes "at the end of the land" that my message for America first began to be birthed, much of it rooted in my ancestors' engagement with the natural world.

Over thousands of years, they had learned to live in concert with the ever-changing moods of the sea and the cycle of the seasons while also taking advantage of the abundant natural resources common to the region; chief among these was the salmon that return to their rivers of origin.

Scarred and bruised from having spent as many as seven years far out at sea chasing herring, shrimp, and anchovies while also evading their pursuers—killer whales, sharks, seals, sea lions, and even fishermen like me—the fully mature survivors of this gauntlet of predators return home to spawn.

Summoning their remaining reserves, the salmon gather around the mouths of their rivers of origin awaiting the fall rains to increase the depths of the rivers sufficient for them to navigate around boulders and fallen trees to the place where, as little smolts (fingerlings), their life began.

There in the shadows of the thick forests and low-lying underbrush that crowd the meandering rivers, the females eventually find a suitable place to lay their eggs and the males fertilize them, ensuring the next generation.

Their mission completed, the adult salmon, emaciated and near death, settle to the river bottom, breathe their last, and with a final quiver of their tail, offer a final sacrifice.

In death, their deteriorating carcasses provide the necessary nutrients their offspring need to survive. And once again the cycle of the seasons from birth to life to death our Creator long ago set in motion continues into the next generation.

Meanwhile, the fast-flowing rivers and streams that had been their home hurry down and around hill and valley past boulders and fallen trees only to lose their identity in the vast Pacific Ocean. But it only seems that way. Eventually the rivers too return in the form of rain. Once again it is the cycle of life established by the Creator.

We can take something positive from this. Because of God's promise, we can be assured that despite the dismal predictions by some that Mother Nature is going to end soon due to global warming or some other natural catastrophe, we can find comfort in knowing the cycle of the seasons and the earth itself will continue until Jesus returns and a new heaven and new earth are created.

Until the day when Jesus returns, we have this assurance in Genesis 8:22: "As long as the earth endures, seedtime and harvest, cold and heat, summer and winter, day and night will never cease."

The writer of the psalm acknowledges,

> Your faithfulness continues through all generations;
> you established the earth and it endures. Your laws
> endure to this day, for all things serve you. (Psalm
> 119:90–91)

Everything the Creator has made, whether the tiniest particles that make up the universe or the vast universe with its trillions of galaxies and stars, is subservient to Him.

11

In Awe of Our Creator

In the beginning was the Word, and the Word was
with God, and the Word was God. He was with God
in the beginning. Through him all things were made;
without him nothing was made that has been made.
—John 1:1-3

DESPITE THE SAD HISTORY OF CHRISTIANITY CORRUPTED WITH
Aristotle's ideas concerning lords and masters, civilized and
barbarians, and the theft of my people's lands, I had an open mind
about the Christian God. And so did many of the elders of my
youth, some of whom had converted to Christianity as result of early
missionary efforts among my people. My maternal grandmother,
Alice, was one of those who did. I wasn't a quick study though.

I occasionally attended Sunday school with a friend. But our
attendance was sporadic at best. Except during the Christmas season,
because that meant Santa Claus was coming to town. The church I
occasionally attended always held a big Christmas party for the entire
community. With a beautiful evergreen set in the sanctuary and gifts
for children under the tree, it was an event all of us children looked
forward to. We believed Santa was real. And every year someone from
the community dressed in a Santa suit would suddenly appear from
a backdoor entrance. In the crush of excited kids pressing against
him, some managed to reach out and grab hold of his gloved hand.
On one occasion, I accidentally pulled his glove back just far enough

so that I could see his hand was brown like mine. Santa, it turns out, was an Indian.

Because my attendance at Sunday school was so infrequent and my attention span minimal, I never learned much about the Creator. Mostly, my Sunday school classmates and I would distract our teacher, a war veteran, and get him to talk about anything but the lessons we were supposed to learn. God had to find another way to get my attention.

The first time I began to sense that there was God occurred in an unusual way: while all alone in the darkness of my bedroom. For reasons I cannot fully explain, I was always afraid of being alone in the dark. Looking back, I suspect demon influence might have been at the root of my fear of the dark. Doors would open and lights would be turned on mysteriously in the back bedroom of our house. This occurred after an old man who my mother took in died while staying in that room. That eventually became my room.

But on this one occasion while home alone and hiding under the covers of my bed, a warm feeling suddenly seemed to engulf the entire room, me included. It was a good feeling. Somehow I understood there was God! Only seven at the time, the sense I had of a powerful, loving God seemed to banish the darkness while preparing me for all that would follow.

This unusual experience was further reinforced while fishing along the banks of the rivers or exploring the beautiful, expansive sand beaches that frame my homeland—initially, the Creator's immense power and glory. Naturally, the vast ocean with all its moods was a good reminder of how small we humans really are.

In later years while accompanying my father on his commercial salmon fishing vessel, *The Benita*, I was especially struck by the rugged nature of the coastline and the jagged rock formations that rose abruptly out of the sea with colorful names like Seal and Sail rock, Father and Son, Ozette Rocks, Pompey's Pillar, Skagway, Strawberry Rock, Slant Rock, Mushroom Rock, etc.

It has been many years since those carefree days of waking long before dawn and then stumbling in the darkness on my way to the place where my father's vessel was moored. But once on his boat, the brisk morning dawn and a numbing cold wind in my face would awaken my senses to marvelous scenes.

Ploughing through ocean swells along a coastline so rugged and uneven that it seemed as if it had been carved by a dull knife inspired a sense of awe.

Looking toward the distant mountains, where vast evergreen forests stood defiantly against the incessant on shore winds, and below where rivers flowed toward spacious sand beaches strewn with weathered logs, kelp, and seaweed, all were visual reminders attesting to the powerful storms of winter that could stir placid seas into a hostile, angry froth. Many a vessel had been overwhelmed by large waves, powerful winds, and dangerous rocks hidden just below the surface of the sea.

The many moods of the North Pacific spoke of beauty and the beast, of blessing and curses, of calm and storm, the way of life. So a question began to form in my mind. *Why the seemingly mixed messages of creation?*

I may never have pursued these questions much further had it not been for an unexpected event that occurred in a most unlikely place. A place far different from the reservation community where I grew up.

As a young teen in 1962, my family decided to attend the Seattle World's Fair, one of the last of the great world fairs held in America. By this time, we had just moved from the reservation to the city of Tacoma and as a young Native boy just off the reservation, I was still trying to adapt to modern city life while forming a broader view of the world. And what I was seeing was not very encouraging.

The world fair's optimistic theme of wondrous innovations to come in the twenty-first century seemed unlikely to ever become a reality given the actual state of the world in 1962.

People thought Armageddon was about to be unleashed. And this was made likely since the very thing the fair highlighted—technological innovation and a wondrous future world—were threatened by the development of horrific weapons of mass destruction that could destroy the entire world.

Once again, the contrast between things good (technology) and evil (the misuse of technology) was in direct conflict. Especially with the advent of the hydrogen bomb and intercontinental ballistic missiles, worldwide catastrophes not only seemed possible but in 1962 very likely.

12

The World on the Brink

For the secret power of lawlessness is already
at work; but the one who now holds it back will
continue to do so till he is taken out of the way.
—2 Thessalonians 2:7

THE 1962 SEATTLE WORLD'S FAIR TOOK PLACE AT A TIME WHEN the Cuban Missile Crisis was about to insert itself as the lead story in newspapers and television newscasts around the world. Evil was poised to be unleashed upon humankind and the entirety of Mother Earth was threatened with destruction.

It was during the summer of that year that the Soviet Union had secretly begun carrying out plans to place medium-range ballistic missiles tipped with nuclear warheads on Cuban soil, barely ninety miles from the US mainland. Along with the missiles, they had also managed to place combat troops on the island.

One truth seems always to be characteristic of nations, perhaps especially those who have a long history of conflict with other nations like Russia and even our nation: fear and self-preservation seem to drive foreign policy objectives.

In October 1962, a US reconnaissance plane flying over Cuba captured images of missiles being offloaded from Soviet cargo ships and then being assembled on Cuban soil.

Seeing evidence of this led to an immediate crisis. What would America do in response? Clearly these missiles were a direct threat to American security and a violation of the Monroe Doctrine, which limited foreign influence in South America.

President John F. Kennedy appeared on television to announce to the nation that he had ordered an immediate naval blockade to ensure that no further Soviet ships were allowed to enter Cuban ports.

In this highly volatile and toxic atmosphere, all that was needed to set off worldwide catastrophe was the tiniest spark.

Intense negotiations began between President Kennedy and Soviet Premier Nikita S. Khrushchev; all the while, mobilization of troops, naval ships, and aircraft of both countries were accelerating at a dangerous pace. This resulted in what became a standoff between the two most powerful nations in the world.

During this intensely stressful time in world history, there were moments when the two nations came close to launching nuclear-tipped missiles against one another.

Several incidents especially stood out during the heightened tensions. One occurred when several senior officers aboard a Soviet submarine identified as B-59 believed they were under attack by US Navy surface ships that unknown to the Soviet commanders, were dropping nonlethal, low-yield depth charges to force the submarine to the surface. The Soviets hearing the noise in their submerged submarine assumed they were under attack.

Unable to contact their homeland to determine whether World War III had already begun, two of three senior officers aboard the submarine decided it was necessary to launch a nuclear-tipped torpedo against the US Navy surface ships. Similar in yield to the Hiroshima bomb, it would have destroyed the ships of America's Atlantic fleet.

Since the Soviet fail-safe procedure required all three senior officers to agree before launching their torpedo, a single officer, Vasili Arkhipov, refused to go along with the other two. Known for being calm under duress, he did not believe the situation merited a nuclear response. The Americans were just trying to persuade the submarine to surface. It is generally understood Arkhipov's refusal to agree with his comrades likely prevented a nuclear holocaust as the US military is said to have targeted the Soviet Union with three thousand nuclear warheads. You can imagine the destructive force an all-out nuclear war would have meant to the entire world. Had a horrible event like this happened, the survivors of a nuclear holocaust would still be trying to restart civilization.

Eventually, the Soviet submarine surfaced amid US naval ships and was allowed to return safely to its homeport.

The decision on the part of a single Soviet naval officer to prevent the launch of a nuclear-tipped torpedo against US Naval surface ships saved the world.

The Soviet officer, Vasili Arkhipov, who wisely concluded their submarine was not under attack was eventually recognized by the Soviets for his part in preventing World War III. He died on August 19, 1998, little noted or recognized by most people for his unique contribution in preventing potential worldwide disaster.

There were other close calls as well, including an accidental intrusion deep into Soviet airspace by Captain John Maultsby, who on October 27, 1962, was flying s U-2 spy plane on a mission that would take him over the North Pole. The pilot's ability to navigate was impaired in part due to the aurora borealis resulting in his plane turning toward the Soviet Union. As the U-2 accidentally strayed into Soviet airspace, the Soviets concluded that this was a hostile act and launched at least six interceptors to shoot it down.

So great was the inherent danger associated with this accidental intrusion into Soviet territory that historian turned Kennedy aide Arthur Schlesinger would later describe this moment as "the most dangerous moment in human history." Soviet missiles in Cuba were already armed and ready to be launched against US cities only a short distance away. And as I had noted, the US military had prepared to launch three thousand nuclear-tipped warheads at Soviet targets.[3]

---

[3] *Vanity Fair*, June 2008, 146, a condensation of the book *One Minute to Midnight*, by author Michael Dobs.

Fortunately, the pilot managed to discover the error in time and was able, despite being low on fuel, to elude the Soviet interceptors long enough to fly his jet safely back to US airspace in Alaska, where he managed to bring his plane to a soft landing at a US military base. Thankfully he survived. And by extension, so did we. An event like this came close to being interpreted by the Soviets as a hostile act, a precursor to an American attack on the Soviet Union.

We may never know how many additional close calls there have been during the era of the Cuban missile crisis or in all the years since that could have resulted in worldwide nuclear annihilation.

Here is the sad truth: given the state of tensions today in the world and the proliferation of nuclear weaponry—currently 9 countries have nuclear weapons and now the development of deadly viruses—the world is far more dangerous than it was in the 1960s.

One thing different in our world today from the dangers America faced in the 1960s is people then were nowhere near as politically divided as we are today.

Moreover, people were generally more religious and Democrats and Republicans were more alike in their values. And for the most part, they refused to politicize moral issues, such as same-sex marriage, gay rights, or abortion. And people could pray in public places to a God they believed would deliver them from evil.

What we can learn from earlier generations and find some comfort during this present age of crises is this: regardless of the threats unfolding in the world and the evil that exists all around us, our Sovereign God is ultimately in control of the outcomes—especially so when things seem most chaotic and out of control.

Behind the scenes of today's headlines, our Creator works to frustrate evil conspiracies to ensure that everything that occurs in this world, whether good or evil, will ultimately accomplish His purposes. He is after all sovereign over the world of politics as well, and that includes nations and their rulers. We read in Isaiah 14:24, "The Lord Almighty has sworn, Surely, as I have planned, so it will be, and as I have purposed, so it will happen."

Ensuring that all happens in accord with His will is the Holy Spirit, the Third Person of the Holy Trinity, who moment by moment constrains the evil men imagine as well as the natural world's most dangerous manifestations.

He will do so until such a time described as the last days, when according to the Bible He is removed "and the lawless one," Satan will be revealed for all the evil he has been doing behind the scenes of history. With Satan unleashed at the end-time, there will be great evil, lies will seem to gain the upper hand over truth, and all that is good will appear to have been lost. Are we there now? I don't know, but it sure seems like it. But here is the good news: evil won't triumph for long.

When Jesus returns, Satan and his demon angels will be annihilated by "the manifestation of His coming." In 2 Thessalonians 2:7–8, we read,

> For the secret power of lawlessness is already at work; but the one who now holds it back will continue to do so till he is taken out of the way. And then the lawless one will be revealed, whom the Lord Jesus will overthrow with the breath of his mouth and destroy by the splendor of his coming.

So we can take courage. Ultimately truth and justice will prevail, good will triumph over evil, and Jesus will be exalted in all His glory. And Satan and his demon followers will be condemned forever to the lake of burning fire, the place we call hell. You can be certain a day of accounting is coming.

At the time Jesus appears in all His glory, every knee will bow, and every tongue will confess that He is Lord, even those who despised or ignored him throughout their lives.

But we are not to be misled by this end-time scene; even though it appears as if there is a revival and everyone becomes a believer in

Jesus, only those who have trusted in Him during their earthly life will be taken into His presence.

Those who ignored or opposed Him throughout their lives will be forever condemned to a place of darkness and despair where they will forever regret not believing in Him as their Savior. Please don't forgo your opportunity to become a disciple of Jesus.

The time to receive Jesus as Savior is now, not when it is too late.

13

Meeting Jesus

The Son is the image of the invisible God,
the firstborn over all creation. For in him all
things were created: things in heaven and on
earth, visible and invisible, whether thrones
or powers or rulers or authorities; all things
have been created through him and for him.
—Colossians 1:15–16

WITH AMERICA AND THE SOVIET UNION ON A COLLISION COURSE leading to the possibility of nuclear war, many Americans in the 1960s were sure that the world was going to come to a horrific end.

Some with the financial means were so convinced of imminent doom they constructed underground bomb shelters in their backyards, stocking them with enough supplies of food, water, and medicines to last for weeks.

As a teenager living in Tacoma following a move from the reservation, I recall working for a wealthy older woman who had one installed in her backyard. One of my duties, besides mowing her lawn, raking leaves, and even washing her sheets, was to climb down a ladder leading to her underground fallout shelter and then manually cranking an air circulator to purify the atmosphere.

How this lady who used a walker to make it around her home, and whose husband, a high-ranking military officer who had died years earlier, expected to survive a postnuclear world was beyond me.

But that was the world that was in 1962, fearful, a little insane, and anticipating the possibility of a nuclear holocaust. As an avid news junky, I was fearful too.

However, on the hot July 8 day that my family chose to attend the Seattle World's Fair, the problems facing our nation and world were far from my mind.

As we approached the turnstiles of the fairgrounds, the exotic smells of food concessions wafting in the air along with the joyous sounds of excited fairgoers inspired anticipation of a wonderful day of fun and discovery.

Everywhere were exhibits from a variety of nations promoting inventions that promised the good life, the result of futuristic innovations that included cars that could fly, machines that could think, portable phones you could carry, cities with elevated monorails to facilitate mass transit, and the promise of space flight to Mars and the rest of the planets.

Like the futuristic Space Needle restaurant towering six hundred feet above the fairgrounds, things on that July day were looking up.

Naturally, as I passed through the turnstiles, I was anxious to experience the promise of a better world to come.

However, just as I was about to strike out for the first display, a person standing at the entrance caught my attention and handed me a bookmark-size invitation to hear Reverend Billy Graham later that day in a smallish, by today's standards, football stadium situated right in the middle of the fairgrounds. July 8 was the famous evangelist's only appearance at the fair.

Interested in hearing Billy Graham's message about the future of the world, I persuaded my parents to allow me to attend.

Somewhat surprised that I would choose a sermon over the enticements of the fair, they reluctantly agreed to let me go alone after I assured them I would meet them at a specified location following the service.

That afternoon, I found myself sitting midway up the stadium while patiently waiting to hear what the famous evangelist had to say.

Soon after stepping up to the podium, Billy Graham, his Southern drawl, powerful voice, and deep-set eyes conveying conviction, began relating how dangerous the world had become and how Jesus was the only one who could save us and our world from certain catastrophe.

He went on to proclaim that each person needed to acknowledge their sinfulness, invite Jesus into their hearts to receive forgiveness of sins, and be assured of eternal life. He repeatedly encouraged his congregation that now was the time to do so. Delay could mean we might miss the opportunity. The Spirit of God might not always be so near or speak so clearly as that moment.

Reminded how dangerous the world outside the fairgrounds had become and convinced in my heart that God was speaking to me through this preacher, after wavering back and forth for a few moments, I finally rose from my seat and walked gingerly down the stadium steps to the field below.

Once on the field, a counselor, a young Asian man, met me and led me in a prayer to invite Jesus into my heart. There were no flashing lights or thunder from the heavens accompanying this moment. But somehow, in the quiet places of my inner being, I knew something had changed in me; Jesus was now my Lord and Savior.

My parents were skeptical at first but eventually accepted the fact that indeed something about me was different. Their first clue had to have been the grin on my face when I approached them.

Shortly thereafter, I began in earnest to study the Bible to learn more about Jesus and what He had accomplished.

It was during these times that I began to understand that Jesus was the Creator, the Second Person of the Holy Trinity who not only spoke the world and the universe into existence—things visible and things invisible—but moment by moment sustains all that He has made.

Quite simply everything in the universe, from the tiniest subatomic particles that make up everything, would fly apart if Jesus did not hold them together. As Colossians 1:15–17 declares concerning Jesus,

The Son is the image of the invisible God, the firstborn over all creation. For in him all things were created: things in heaven and on earth, visible and invisible, whether thrones or powers or rulers or authorities; all things have been created through him and for him.

As I began to understand more of the Bible, it became clear Jesus wasn't just a baby born in the manger who did some good things once. He was far greater than I had ever imagined. He was the Son of God, the Light of the World, and the Creator and Sustainer of all things big and small.

For the first time I could begin to appreciate the Creator of everything I had witnessed in the wondrous scenes of my childhood and why it was important to follow Him.

A few weeks following my encounter with Jesus, I felt the call on my life to put God first. I was just sixteen when the Holy Spirit began nudging me to enter the ministry.

The sense I had of His call on my life reached a critical moment when a respected elder from my community, who had heard of my coming to faith at a Billy Graham meeting, encouraged me to become a minister. Looking intently into my eyes, she said, "You need to go into the ministry so you can help your people."

At first, I strongly resisted the idea. Many Native Americans, because of the unjust treatment they had endured during the founding of America, were resistant to Christianity. For them, Jesus was the White man's God, a deception Satan was only too willing to encourage among Native people across America.

That was not my issue. I just had other ideas for my life, and becoming a pastor was certainly not one of them.

Despite this, so compelling was the inner call on my life that I was convinced I had to do whatever the Spirit of God called on me to do. With that as my new direction in life, I began to study the scriptures more intently.

14

A Tragic Secret

Prior to my coming to faith in Jesus and while still residing on the Makah reservation, my mother and father had little to do with the Christian faith. I am not sure why since their parents, especially my grandmother on my mother's side, was known for being a caring Christian always on the lookout to help the needy.

My father had Christian parents too, but friends he worked with when he was young persuaded him to start drinking. At times, my father invited his drinking buddies to come over to our home despite my mother's desperate pleadings to the contrary. She knew this created a very unhealthy atmosphere for us kids. At times, to protect us, she hid us in a closet. Eventually my mother had had enough. She began divorce proceedings. It led to a bitter family conflict and deep wounds on both sides.

My father's alcoholism and their contentious divorce left both parents angry and bitter throughout the rest of their lives.

Frequently vying for our loyalty since we lived with our mother and our father resided only blocks away, we children were torn apart emotionally.

Both of our parents eventually married other partners. However, the pain of their divorce impacted me and my siblings for many years thereafter. Our broken family, however, was not the only issue.

There was another problem. Something horrific had occurred in my mother's childhood that left deep emotional scars that plagued her throughout much of her life. Even as a child I sensed this but didn't know what it was.

Then shortly before her death due to kidney failure, I had a troubling conversation with her. My mother's failing kidneys were traceable years earlier to a time when my older brother, Leonard, contracted rheumatic fever.

Confined to homecare for well over a year, he lost precious school time and never did learn to read or write until after we left the reservation, and he was afforded remedial education in a public school in Tacoma.

During his confinement at home and while under the constant care of my mother, her kidneys became infected, something she managed to live with for a time.

When her condition worsened, friends in the community encouraged her to see a doctor. The news was not good. Her doctor indicated she didn't have much time to live and suggested she return home and use her remaining time to put her affairs in order.

Only seven at the time, I remember the somber hour-and-a-half ride home following her visit with the doctor. Halfway there, my mother, her face ashen, turned to my brother and me sitting quietly in the back seat of the car and, with subdued voice cracking with emotion, began to tell us how we needed to look out for each other. She implied that she wasn't going to be around much longer.

Unable to grasp her meaning, I sat in puzzled silence, conscious only of the world outside my window receding with each passing moment.

Once we arrived at our home on the reservation, word spread quickly around the community concerning my mother's dire condition.

The next day a trusted elder familiar with ancient Indian cures brought my mother a big pot of tea made of the boiled bark of a crab apple tree that grew wild in the area. Bitter to the taste, the tea was not something you would drink unless you were desperate. But what a wonderful cure for internal infections. It helped to cure my acne when I was a kid.

My mother faithfully stuck with the daily regimen the elder had prescribed, drinking a full glass of the bitter-tasting tea three times a day.

Amazingly, when she returned for a follow-up visit with her doctor a month later, her kidney infection was greatly diminished. "What happened?" her bewildered doctor asked. "I thought you would be dead by now." For the next forty years, my mother lived with 40 percent of her kidney function.

But then in her midseventies, a fall down a basement stairway caused her to be hospitalized and given medication. Whatever they administered triggered her already weakened kidneys to begin to completely fail. Placed on dialysis, her health quickly deteriorated.

Living in another state while serving in the ministry made visiting her on a regular basis difficult. But whenever possible, I would go to her side.

One day, realizing she did not have much time, I was able to arrange another visit. By now her formerly dark hair had turned white, her body, a mere shadow of its former self left her fragile and weak. Communication was halting and obviously painful for her. Nevertheless, she was happy to see me.

Toward the end of what was to be the last time I would see her, she began to sob. It made me uncomfortable. "Mom," I said, "is there anything I can do to help?"

It was then that she blurted out something like "I was standing in the doorway when the doctor removed the baby from my mother's womb."

What? I was taken aback. I had always known something tragic had happened to her family in the past. The deadly procedure had been a family taboo so painful no one in her family would talk about it. Now at the end of her life, she felt compelled to tell me, her pastor son, what had happened. But why was this on her heart at such a difficult time in her own life?

15

A Deadly Procedure

When rapid change takes place, the deeper it
goes, the more disturbing and upsetting it is
to everything. It casts a dark shadow over the
whole of one's life ... it invalidates and obliterates
everything the person has known or believed.
—Dr. Lee Griffin, psychiatrist

THE TRAGIC SCENE MY MOTHER WAS ABOUT TO DESCRIBE WAS SO
traumatic for her and her siblings that it cast a dark shadow over all
the rest of their lives, obliterating the peace and security they had
known. In muted tones, my mother began to explain what had led to
her mother's death and that of the child she was carrying.

In the final stages of her mother's pregnancy, the little child
they decided to name Phyllis had at the last moment turned in the
womb. In the 1930s when this occurred, Indian tribes were subject
to extensive government administration that included their health
care, education, law and order, and jurisdiction over all reservation
land. As previously related, long before progressives began to promote
socialism in America, an early form of it was already being imposed
on Native tribes.

To enforce socialistic policies and cause Native Americans to
conform to a new way of life, government agents, teachers, and health
care interns were assigned to Native American communities with

little professional experience or understanding of Native culture or their needs.

Since the child in my grandmother's womb was breech, someone contacted the local intern doctor assigned to the community. He immediately came to their little home.

Bordering on incompetent, the intern made the fateful decision to forcefully extract the child. Using forceps, he succeeded in removing the baby girl, killing the tiny child while also severely injuring my grandmother. During her agony, she also began losing blood.

You can imagine the gruesome scene unfolding: a mother screaming in pain, a tiny child lying limp next to her, and the adults around the bed horrified.

Amid the chaos of this badly botched procedure, no one noticed the young girl standing in the doorway of the small bedroom watching intently as the tragic procedure was taking place. It was my mother.

Anyone who witnesses something so traumatizing, especially a child, cannot help but be adversely affected. Many may assume false guilt as if they had something to do with it.

In the case of my mother, it was obvious that the cruel event left her with deep emotional scars that followed her throughout her life.

I recall times when she would break down and cry for no apparent reason. Sometimes in an obvious state of sadness, she would stare off in evident despair. It may also explain why she seemed always to be looking for an elder in the community to be her mother.

The loss of the little child and not long after her mother had devastating impacts on her siblings as well. Each in their own way processed their pain in different ways.

One elder who had been a surrogate mother to my mom seemed to fill that role, but she abruptly left the community, leaving my mother desperately sad.

Naturally my grandfather was especially devastated. He had to be restrained by the men of the community from taking vengeance on the incompetent intern.

During his unbearable grief, he managed to arrange transport by boat for his wife now barely clinging to life. The nearest hospital was in the small city of Port Angeles, a four-hour boat ride up the strait from their home.

However, they were turned away by the hospital authorities who reasoned that she should instead go to the Cushman Indian hospital in Tacoma to receive treatment. Were they prejudiced against Indians? I don't know the answer. What I do know is that lacking timely care, she died soon after arriving in Tacoma.

Shortly after returning home following his beloved wife's death, my grandfather borrowed a tractor and with it bulldozed his house to the ground and then set it afire.

It is said that he believed evil spirits conspired with the incompetence of the intern to harm his family. I suspect he was right.

Once I understood the full scope of this horrific tragedy, it had a profound impact on me. I began to understand how family traumas can be passed from generation to generation. Abortion, whether accidental or intentional, has long-term effects on the individual, the family, and yes, even a nation.

Nevertheless, I am convinced God in His grace is always willing to heal the wounds. My heart goes out to all the mothers and their families who have had to deal with the guilt and shame many of them feel following abortion. And I know that God loves and forgives and can bring healing to them.

On the other hand, a nation or state that condones and encourages abortion will face certain judgment, not somewhere down the road but now. Already God's wrath is being visited upon our nation for this grievous sin.

16

The World without You

GOD HAD GRACIOUSLY INTERVENED IN MY LIFE, ENABLING ME TO rise above the circumstances that so traumatized my family. It wasn't easy though. I struggled with issues of self-confidence, and my mother's anxieties were passed on to me. In some small way, her pain had become my own.

However sad my family's experience with this tragedy had been though, it was something God would eventually use in my life. I saw up close what the trauma of an abortion could do to a family and how it affected me, a generation removed from the event.

However, it would take years before I would finally begin to process the event. When I accepted the call into ministry in the 1960s, Roe versus Wade was not yet the law of the land. I graduated from seminary in 1973, the same year it was adopted by the US Supreme Court.

Eventually, as I read the Bible, I began to understand that God never wants an abortion to end the life of a child in the womb, although in rare cases where the mother's life is in danger, that might be necessary.

However, this was not the situation in my family; it was a procedure gone bad. Unintentional perhaps, but the effects were the same. Lost lives, an abiding sense of guilt and shame, and a deep sense of loss.

My grandfather, as I mentioned, had a sense that behind the scenes of his family's tragedy, evil spirits were somehow involved. I suspect the spirit of the ancient Amorite god Molech, who was identified in ancient times with child sacrifice, is behind abortion.

Laws in this nation that affirm the reproductive rights of woman to end a pregnancy and that emphasize a woman's right to choose may sound good. But it is the modern-day equivalent of child sacrifice, and that has incredible emotional impacts on a family, as my mother's story illustrates. But there is another consequence no one talks about—the cost to a nation when so many children are lost.

How does a nation account for over 70 million children sacrificed to abortion? We will never know what blessings these innocent children might have brought to their families, their communities, and our nation. Their loss invites a question you can ask of yourself. "What if I had never been born?"

Perhaps you know of the 1946 movie by Frank Capra titled *It's a Wonderful Life* and starring James Stewart and Donna Reed.

Considered one of the one hundred greatest movies of all time and now a Christmas classic, it concerned a man played by Stewart who had made many sacrifices to keep a savings and loan bank from closing, thus permitting the townspeople of his hometown of Bedford Falls to keep their investments and allowing them to build businesses and purchase homes. At one point, he saved his future war hero brother from drowning, losing his hearing in one ear in the process. Because of his hearing loss, he was ineligible for military service when WWII broke out.

His was an exemplary life of self-sacrifice, until one day money from the savings and loan he managed was accidentally displaced by a coworker. The character played by Stewart was blamed and faced possible federal charges. So great was his despair that he considered ending his life by jumping into the icy cold river that ran through the middle of the town.

Then, just as he was about to jump off the bridge, an angel intervened. What followed was the angel taking him through scenes that would have taken place in his hometown of Bedford Falls, had he never been born.

None of it was good. Life without him would have been tragic for many people, had he not been there to help his community and family. His brother, a highly decorated WWII hero, would have drowned in childhood never having served in the military. The movie inspires a question for each of us to consider. "What would life be like if you had never been born?" This is a question that will haunt our nation long into the future.

Sadly, this crime against children is not the only offense our nation is committing against children. Tim Ballard, founder of an organization called Operation Underground Railroad and the man portrayed in the highly successful movie *The Sound of Freedom,* which exposes the evils of sex trafficking of children, said in an interview with *Epoch Times,* "The United States is the No. 3 for destination countries for human trafficking and No. 1 for consumption of child rape videos. We are now approaching No. 1 in production of child exploitation material."[4]

The trafficking of children for immoral purposes is an abomination to a holy and righteous God. It cannot go unpunished, and Jesus warned anyone who dares to offend little children. "It would be better for them to be thrown into the sea with a millstone tied around their neck than to cause one of these little ones to stumble" (Luke 17:2).

You can be sure of this: a day of reckoning is coming for all those who deliberately target children for death or exploit for immoral purposes.

---

[4] *Epoch News,* A8, US Edition, July 19–25, 2023.

17

The Cry of Creation

For the creation waits in eager expectation for the
children of God to be revealed. For the creation
was subjected to frustration, not by its own
choice, but by the will of the one who subjected
it, in hope that the creation itself will be liberated
from its bondage to decay and brought into the
freedom and glory of the children of God.
—Romans 18:19–21

As you might imagine, coming from a family that had experienced multiple stresses including alcoholism and divorce, I needed to work through its impacts on me in preparation for the ministry.

And now with God's call on my life following the Billy Graham meeting, my life purpose was becoming clearer. I was intent on helping people find salvation and healing through Jesus, who had come into my life and called me to enter the ministry.

I began to consider the training I would need. Mostly I focused on the educational requirement. No one in my family had ever entered the ministry, much less pursued education beyond grade school.

During this initial period of investigation, I was amazed to learn that the state of sin I experienced, and creation's often chaotic and unpredictable manifestations I had witnessed while growing up, were directly related to our first parents, Adam and Eve, who had disobeyed God by eating fruit from the tree of knowledge of good and evil. God had explicitly commanded them not to do that.

The consequences for disobeying His command were unequivocal.

> You are free to eat from any tree in the garden; but you must not eat from the tree of the knowledge of good and evil, for when you eat from it you will certainly die. (Genesis 2:16–18)

This meant not only would they experience physical death but spiritual death as well. But it didn't end there. Because of their disobedience, God placed a curse upon the things He had made, not because the natural world sinned but because our first parents did. God declared to Adam, "Cursed is the ground because of you; through painful toil you will eat food from it all the days of your life" (Genesis 3:17). To Eve He declared, "I will make your pains in childbearing very severe; with painful labor you will give birth to children. Your desire will be for your husband and he will rule over you" (Genesis 3:16).

Creation and humankind after the Fall were now engaged in a monumental struggle. No longer experiencing a harmonious relationship, making a living in a post-Fall world would be more difficult. Childbearing would also reflect this struggle, the pain reflecting the need from conception to birth, to depend on our Creator God.

All of creation was now subject to mortality and unpredictability. And humans, by their careless stewardship of things created, would contribute if not accelerate the tendency for it to become destructive, often resulting in the extinction of entire species of animals, birds, and fish.

One of the ways this was illustrated to me in my youth was the often difficult challenge of making a living fishing for salmon on the ocean.

"The end of the land where the birds gather" was notorious for powerful storms, rough seas, bitterly cold winds, and especially in the winter months, dark and gloomy skies that lingered sometimes for weeks. Through the years, more than a few vessels were lost at sea because of extreme weather conditions. This made commercial fishing dangerous, strenuous, and risky at times due to fog, bad weather, and accompanying rough seas.

Then there were those occasions when the fish were scarce. Fish populations, especially salmon, were highly susceptible to overharvesting as well as a variety of environmental conditions, including ocean warming during an El Nino (warm water displaced from the south), pollution, depletion of the tiny krill that was part of the food cycle, or any number of other hard to predict factors.

My father who for most of his life had fished commercially for salmon, cod, and halibut was especially adept at reading the signs in nature and forecasting likely outcomes. As an example, he predicted the end of a species of a fish that had for eons of time provided my people with food.

Columbia River wild king salmon, as opposed to hatchery-born salmon, were typically stronger and larger and had a brownish-green color along their backs that distinguished them from other salmon. By the middle of the 1960s, however, there were noticeably fewer of these and most eventually disappeared from the ocean. My father was right.

One of the major reasons for their disappearance was hydroelectric dams, a primary source for America's growing energy needs.

Poor design of passageways was the problem; it did not permit salmon returning to the Columbia River following their ocean sojourn to make it past the turbines on their way to their spawning areas.

Ever since it came under the curse of the Fall, all of creation has been subject to human abuse and carelessness along with its own tendency to become unpredictable.

According to the Word of God, all of creation is experiencing "frustration" or "futility" and we have had to endure the consequences. Moreover, in what is a mystery, it longs for freedom from bondage to decay and chaos. Roman 8:19 affirms, "Everything You have created eagerly waits in expectation of the time when Your children will appear in their full and final glory."

This is an inconvenient truth people in our environmentally conscious culture are unaware of or choose to ignore: that all of creation responds to the Creator and is somehow aware that it can never be free from its bondage to sin and decay until Jesus returns.

And here is another inconvenient truth: the increase in all its disruptive manifestations, including the disappearance of entire species of fish and animals, has become more pronounced in concert with the world becoming more wicked as we approach the end of time.

This has led me to the further conclusion that the natural world's behavior is due more to our disobedience to our Creator than all the things we have done as careless stewards of the environment.

Moreover, its often dangerous manifestations, including devastating earthquakes, tornadoes, and vicious storms, are evidence of a desperate longing to be freed from the curse pronounced upon it by the Creator. But it knows it cannot be freed until the children of God "are revealed in their full glory," a reference to the return of Jesus when he will resurrect his children to a glorious new existence.

Mother Nature is not alone in its desperate pleadings to be freed from the curse of mortality. Our physical bodies, also part of creation, experience similar signs of the curse, especially as we age.

Like the rest of creation, our bodies long for the same deliverance the natural world longs for: freedom from a myriad of illnesses and especially freedom from mortality and eventual death.

That said, while we live in this world, we are to be responsible stewards of Jesus's creation, and that includes taking care of our physical bodies by eating the right foods, exercising regularly, and going for regular checkups with our doctor. That we can all agree.

But we must also understand this: a right relationship with the natural world begins first and foremost with a right relationship with our Creator.

And that means experiencing a faith relationship with Jesus, the Creator and Sustainer of all things, and having an appreciation for all He has done for us.

Unfortunately, we Americans are seeing a decline in respect for our Creator, and that is problematic because nature somehow senses this and reacts to our turning away from our Creator by becoming more disruptive and unpredictable.

18

Trending Away from God

The wrath of God is being revealed from heaven
against all the godlessness and wickedness of
people, who suppress the truth by their wickedness.
—Romans 1:18

WHILE MOST AMERICANS CONTINUE TO AFFIRM BELIEF IN GOD, AS
many as 50 percent claim not to have any denominational affiliation,
the lowest since records have been kept (according to a Fox News
Poll in 2023).

The seven mainline Christian Protestant churches are the United
Methodist Church, the Evangelical Lutheran Church in America,
the United Church of Christ, the Presbyterian Church USA, the
American Baptist Church, the Episcopal Church, and the Christian
Church Disciples of Christ; all have seen major declines in church
attendance, especially since the 1970s, as many of the younger
generation no longer see the relevance of church attendance.

My denominational affiliation, the Lutheran Church Missouri
Synod, conservative by comparison to the mainline denominations,
had in the early 1970s about 3 million members. Today, only 1.8
million consider themselves to be part of the denomination.

According to a Pew Research Pole conducted in 2015, Mainline
Protestants have one of the lowest retention rates of any major
religious tradition, with only 45 percent of those raised in the faith
continuing in it after becoming adults.

With this trend downward, according to another Pew Research poll taken in 2022, it has been estimated that by 2070, less than 50 percent of Americans will claim to be Christian.

More recently, according to a *Wall Street Journal* poll taken in March 2023, of 1019 adults surveyed to determine which values were most important, respondents rated patriotism at 38 percent compared to 70 percent in a similar 1998 poll; religious faith was 39 percent compared to 62 percent in the same poll.

It is even worse in Europe, where a similar poll taken by Pew Research between April and August 2017 reveals that only 18 percent of the population attend church one or more times a month.

The abandonment of traditional values, especially spiritual ones, has led to massive culture shifts in Europe and America.

To see how rapidly this has occurred and its effects on morality, one need only examine how cultural values have changed since the 1960s.

19

The Rising Tide of Nihilism

Seduction, subversion, sedition—these are the tools
of a creature we once called Satan, the father of lies,
the loser of the Battle in Heaven. Yet he continues
to fight here on earth with the only weapons at his
disposal: man's inherent weaknesses and zeal to
be duped if the cause seems appealing enough.
—Michael Walsh, *The Devil's Pleasure Palace*

IF YOU WERE RAISED IN THE 1950S AND 1960S, YOU WOULD HAVE fond memories of a more optimistic time, an era when our nation, despite many challenges, was united politically and to some degree religiously. We rallied around the flag and prayers and Christian symbols were allowed in public schools. Sex trafficking of children was almost unheard of, gender identity issues were never mentioned, crime was mostly under control, people got married before living together, mass shootings were unlikely, and drug problems like the current fentanyl crisis plaguing America were unimaginable. And when people looked out their window and saw a rainbow, they were more likely to think of God's promise never again to destroy the world with floodwaters and not gay rights.

No one in the post-World War II generation thought about defunding the police or supporting radical organizations intent on destabilizing America. And parents were not afraid to let their children play unattended in the community and did not fear that their children in public schools would be exposed to pornography or gender confusion philosophies.

And furthermore, stores did not have to abandon communities because of lawless individuals who looted their businesses and threatened workers or set up homeless camps at their front doors.

It was a time when law and order and Christian values prevailed, and justice for the most part was swift and applied equally, a time that acknowledged past injustices without calling for radical social change or the dismantling of our police. No one dared call for change of the US Constitution. It was a time when most people still acknowledged the importance of God and the rule of law.

Naturally, people growing up in the post-World War II era felt safer in their communities than people today who worry about carjackings or being mugged or assaulted while walking along the streets in their neighborhoods.

But with affluence and the gradual abandonment of God and His righteous laws, baby boomers and succeeding generations began to put God far back in the rearview mirror of their lives. In this new culture of unbelief, nihilism reared its ugly head; a godless philosophy where belief in the relevance of God and His eternal and righteous laws were dismissed. When this idea begins to permeate society, people no longer can explain who they are or why they exist.

There are those who suggest that this was due in part to certain educators who were part of the so-called "Frankfort school" of theologians and philosophers who fled Nazi Germany to America during World War II.

Welcomed to our country during difficult times, they brought with them a Marxist philosophy that through their writings and teachings contaminated the American university system and eventually our children by promising an illusionary world where racism and poverty could be ended and social justice could be achieved by promising a utopian heaven on earth achieved by rejecting past values. Oddly, people of European ancestry seemed most susceptible to these radical philosophies.

Author Michael Walsh, in his book *The Devil's Pleasure Palace*, opined that through a strategy known as critical race theory, Marxists unleashed a horde of demons on the American psyche.[5] The American progressive movement that grew out of the Marxist philosophy gradually began to weave its way into the American culture, undermining many of America's traditional institutions while also discrediting its founders and undermining traditional ideas about the role of Christian values in the formation of the American constitution.

Why were European origin Americans particularly susceptible to such radically different ideas? Michael Walsh, playwright, author, and political columnist, explained.

> Chief among the weaknesses of Western man (Europeans) today is his fundamental lack of cultural self-confidence, his willingness to open his ears to the siren song of nihilism, a juvenile eagerness to believe the worst about himself and his society and to relish on some level, his own prospective destruction.[6]

The willingness on the part of many to embrace socialism is especially dangerous because it affords an open invitation for dark spirits working within the invisible world to influence or even enter the lives of an individual or the nation that no longer acknowledges the Creator or honors His laws. This is a huge problem.

If there is no longer God consciousness and His moral laws are no longer considered relevant, people become little more than vacant souls unable to explain the meaning of their existence or adhere to any moral constraints.

In a nation no longer confident of its former values and its institutions of government eroded because of this, Satan, the

---

[5] Walsh, Michael. *The Devil's Pleasure Palace*. New York: Encounter Books, 2015.
[6] Ibid., 8.

"father of lies," places his imprint on American culture through the very governmental institutions responsible for upholding our laws and protecting us from lawlessness. Sadly, many progressive-leaning churches, because they also have abandoned their former commitment to God and His Word, especially since the 1970s, have approved some of the new societal trends growing out of the rejection of the Creator's moral laws. Rather than challenging the emerging immorality, they have chosen to adapt and even endorse the new culture. Thus, many formally orthodox or Bible-based churches advocate for homosexuality, same-sex marriage, ordination of gay priests or pastors, and even abortion. And many orthodox churches, unwilling to recognize the assault on Christian values or cause conflict among their politically divided parishioners, deliberately avoid speaking the truth lest they lose members.

When Christian churches vacate their former faith, ignore biblical truth, and refuse to carry out their duty to serve as gate keepers of truth, they no longer serve as God's messengers to a nation. And that is problematic not only for the church but also invites the wrath of God. We read these ominous words of warning in Ezekiel 33:8–9 regarding the watchman over the house of Israel:

> If I say to the wicked, O wicked one, you shall surely die, and you do not speak to warn the wicked to turn from his way, that wicked person shall die in his iniquity, but his blood I will require at your hand. But if you warn the wicked to turn from his way, that person will die in his iniquity, but you will have delivered your soul.

20

Our House Swept Clean

When an impure spirit comes out of a person, it
goes through arid places seeking rest and does not
find it. Then it says, "I will return to the house I left."
—Luke 11:24

It was no less than Aristotle, the father of Western civilization, who articulated the physical principle "Nature abhors a vacuum." This appears to apply to the spiritual world as well.

Providing an illustration of the risks associated with rejecting God and the nihilism or emptiness of the soul that results, Jesus related the story of a man who had a demon cast out of him but in response to God's graciousness had done nothing with his opportunity to invite Him into his life. A spiritual void of the soul ensued. The situation Jesus described was comparable to a house that had been "swept clean" but no longer had a tenant.

The demon that had vacated the man, finding no rest in the wilderness places where it had been banished, was allowed to return to its former host, whereupon seeing the emptiness of the man's heart brought with it seven other demons worse than the first so that "the last state of that man was worse than the first."

The lesson is profound. A person without a moral compass and by extension a nation that once honored God and His righteous laws but no longer does so are like a house swept clean. And just as in the physical laws of nature, the void must be filled.

You can understand, based on Jesus's illustration, who will act to fill the void. Demonic forces under Satan's direction are ever on the lookout to wreak havoc in the person or the soul of a nation that no longer acknowledges God or His eternal righteous values. In Romans 1:29–31, the apostle Paul described the result.

> They have become filled with every kind of wickedness, evil, greed and depravity. They are full of envy, murder, strife, deceit, and malice. They are gossips, slanderers, God-haters, insolent, arrogant and boastful; they invent ways of doing evil; they disobey their parents; they have no understanding, no fidelity, no love, no mercy.

Then verse 32 says, "Although they know God's righteous decree that those who do such things deserve death, they not only continue to do these very things but also approve of those who practice them." In Ephesians 6:12, the apostle Paul warns us, "For our struggle is not against flesh and blood, but against the rulers, against the authorities, against the powers of this dark world and against the spiritual forces of evil in the heavenly realms."

Sadly, Romans 1 describes the American scene today, a troubling moral decline that previous generations would never have imagined could occur in their lifetime.

One of the more obvious signs of our moral decline is this generation seems to have lost its sense of right and wrong. When someone speaks out against the immorality of our time or refuses to go along with the new trends, they are labeled racist or prejudiced. It is described as "cancel culture."

When parents attending school board meetings raise their voices in opposition to efforts to teach their children that it is acceptable to change their gender or protest books that violate their morals, they can be arrested and investigated by the FBI as possible terrorists. In summary, what would have appalled previous generations is widely accepted as the norm in our present culture.

And furthermore, because our house is vacant and we have allowed dark spirits to enter and inhabit our rooms, we have created a spiritual environment where demonic forces can encourage evil acts. This has given rise to increasing crime rates and some of its most evil expressions: the senseless mass shooting of innocent children and adults in schools, malls, and other public places.

The perpetrators, often teenagers with troubled pasts, are typically loners who spend a lot of time on the dark side of the internet and may even have some involvement with the occult.

I recall a psychiatrist interviewed following another horrendous mass shooting at one of our nation's public schools; he suggested a motive was the nihilism of this present age.

Troubled individuals who lack self-worth and moral restraints are more likely to be susceptible to committing senseless acts of violence.

This is a biblical principal America needs to understand. When a person or a nation rejects God, His protection from evil influences is withdrawn and Satan is afforded an advantage. And that is not because God no longer loves us, but to the contrary; it is we who no longer love Him.

We read His response to our rebellion in Romans 1:28. "Furthermore, just as they did not think it worthwhile to retain the knowledge of God, so God gave them over to a depraved mind, so that they do what ought not to be done."

Please understand this: When God "gives us up" to our sinful passions and allows Satan to have his way among us, He is not giving up on us. Instead, in His grace amid the troubles we bring upon ourselves, He intends to cause us to acknowledge our sin and repent.

He is always ready to embrace and love us. It is not He who has moved from us but we who have departed from Him.

Our nation's founders understood this far better than our leaders do today. George Washington, this nation's first president, had a premonition of America's future when, during his first inaugural address, he warned future generations of Americans, "A nation that disregards the eternal order and right that heaven itself has ordained" cannot expect the "propitious smiles of heaven." Proverbs 14:34 affirms, "Righteousness exalts a nation, but sin condemns any people."

21

A Lesson from a Minor Prophet

Look at the nations and watch—and be utterly
amazed. For I am going to do something in your day
that you would not believe, even if you were told.
—Habakkuk 1:5

HAVE YOU EVER WONDERED WHY AMERICA, THE PLACE WHERE
opportunity and freedom abound, could so suddenly face the
possibility that it might lose its former place as the leader of the free
world? Or that it might submit to becoming a totalitarian state? With
the gradual loss of freedoms and the way some of our government
agencies are conducting themselves, we seem to be headed in that
direction.

Habakkuk, one of the Twelve Minor Prophets of the Old
Testament, had concerns for his own nation that led him to complain
to God about the conditions taking place in his country.

A member of the tribe of Judah, he was distressed by the moral
decline evident among his people. In desperation, he pleaded to God,

> How long, Lord, must I call for help, but you do
> not listen? Or cry out to you, "Violence!" but you
> do not save? Why do you make me look at injustice?
> Why do you tolerate wrongdoing? Destruction and

violence are before me; there is strife, and conflict abounds. Therefore, the law is paralyzed, and justice never prevails. The wicked hem in the righteous, so that justice is perverted. (Habakkuk 1:2–4)

How similar is this to America today? An unfair justice system, the rise in crime and violence, divisiveness among the electorate, foolish leadership, widespread immorality, racial strife, and the sacrifice of generations of our children to abortion.

The evils Habakkuk witnessed among the people of Judah were directly related to their having turned away from God. Forsaking the faith of their forefathers, they neglected the care of the temple in Jerusalem and turned to the idolatrous worship of false gods including Molech, the detestable god of the Ammonites, a demonic underworld figure who required child sacrifice.

In Jeremiah 32:33–35, we read the progression of their sin leading to child sacrifice.

> They turned their backs to me and not their faces; though I taught them again and again, they would not listen or respond to discipline. They set up their vile images in the house that bears my Name and defiled it. They built high places for Baal in the Valley of Ben Hinnom to sacrifice their sons and daughters to Molech, though I never commanded— nor did it enter my mind—that they should do such a detestable thing and so make Judah sin.

The horrific sins of Judah weren't the only concern of Habakkuk. His people had been conquered and forced into exile by a powerful enemy, the Babylonians, described by God as "a fierce and impetuous nation who march through the breadth of the earth to seize dwellings not their own."

Habakkuk couldn't understand why God would allow a nation more wicked than his own to have dominance over them. Where was the justice in that?

Finally, God chose to respond to Habakkuk. In chapter 1:5–6, we read,

> Look at the nations and watch—and be utterly amazed. For I am going to do something in your days that you would not believe, even if you were told. I am raising up the Babylonians, that ruthless and impetuous people, who sweep across the whole earth to seize dwellings not their own.

What?

Sovereign over every principality, power, and authority, here is the truth Habakkuk had not understood. God had raised up the Babylonian Empire, wicked, idolatrous, and ruthless as it was, to be used as an instrument of His purpose to cause the people of Judah to turn back to Him.

It goes against our sensibilities that God would raise up an evil nation like the Babylonians to achieve His greater good. Our problem is human pride. In our flawed state, we often think we know better than God. However, in Isaiah 55:9, we are reminded, "For as the heavens are higher than the earth, so are my ways higher than your ways, and my thoughts than your thoughts."

In truth, we do not know what God knows or His working among the nations of the world. We don't even know ourselves. That is why we find it surprising when He permits certain circumstances to overtake us.

And since the works of God in our lives and the world around us are beyond our understanding, we must first acknowledge that God knows what He is doing and we don't, and that begins with a spirit of humility. God said to Habakkuk, "See, the enemy is puffed up; his desires are not upright—but the righteous person will live by his faithfulness" (Habakkuk 2:4).

Though we may not understand the workings of God, we are encouraged to set aside our pride and "live by faith," and that means trusting Him no matter the events unfolding daily in our country whether good or bad.

The parallels to Judah to present-day America are striking in their similarity. America was once a bright light of hope and light to the world. God had blessed us immeasurably in so many ways. Our geographical location, bordered by two oceans, served to isolate us from threats. And yet we have turned away from Him.

Now we have the same immorality, the same issues with the lack of truth and justice and increasing violence. And we sacrifice our children (the unborn) just as Judah had done.

And just as in the case of Judah, we have the growing threat of a powerful nation God has allowed to be raised up, the nation of China. Like Babylon of old, they are "a fierce and impetuous nation" that has vowed to displace America as the supreme leader of the world economically, militarily, and politically. Like the Babylonians, they are a godless nation whose crimes against humanity seem worse than our own.

We can't begin to understand all the reasons why God has allowed tensions in the Middle East and China to become so much of a threat to our nation. We simply must recognize the all-encompassing wisdom and power of God and our own shortsightedness and then by faith trust that God, through all the circumstances our nation is currently facing, is doing something incredibly important, something astounding you and I might not believe even if we were told.

What we can know is this: allowing our nation to experience difficulties with our economy, the growing strength of our enemies, and our lack of unity is not intended to harm us but is a part of His divine grace intended to cause us to repent and turn back to Him.

In the case of a nation like Judah, though unfaithful to God and conquered by the Babylonians, God had a plan to cause Judah to return to Him.

What God knew and chose not to tell Habakkuk was that the Babylonians, after two hundred years of ruling over Judah, would themselves be conquered by the Persian Empire, another kingdom God chose to raise up. The Persian king Artaxerxes would show the nation of Judah favoritism and would allow the exiled nation to return to Jerusalem during Nehemiah's time (445–420 BC), affording them the resources and protections needed to rebuild the walls and the freedom to return to their former faith.

A contemporary of Nehemiah, Ezra read the Pentateuch (the first five books of the Bible) to the people. Once they heard God's laws, a great revival followed as the formally rebellious nation repented of their evil ways and began once more to honor God and His righteous laws.

Over the years that followed, the people of Judah would come under the dominance of the Greek Empire and eventually the Roman Empire.

The restoration of the nation of Judah and the eventual rise of the Greek and especially the Roman empires would again subject the Jewish people to subservience. As unlikely as this may have appeared, this prepared the way for Jesus to be born in Bethlehem of Judea and His message of salvation to be spread throughout the whole world.

God could have explained all of this to Habakkuk, but it was more than he needed to know or could possibly understand.

The book of Habakkuk brought to my mind an adage I memorized early in my Christian faith. "When we in darkness walk and no longer feel the heavenly flame, then is the time to trust the Lord and rest upon His name" (author unknown).

Habakkuk went from complaining to God, born of his pride, to embracing Him through faith and finally praising of God in all his circumstances. He learned that no matter the circumstances, he should trust God. Even if we don't understand it at the time, He is doing a work in this time and place and in our individual lives that if we knew all the details would astound us. We might not even believe it if we were told.

One way God encourages us to believe and have faith in all our circumstances is reinforced when Jesus afforded us an insight into the coming birth of a new world to come.

22

Providing an Ultrasound of the World

A woman giving birth to a child has pain
because her time has come; but when her baby
is born, she forgets the anguish because of
her joy that a child is born into the world.
—John 16:21

We know that the whole creation has
been groaning as in the pains of childbirth
right up to the present time.
—Romans 8:22

IT IS NOT ONLY NATIONS AND INDIVIDUALS THAT EXPERIENCE THE
effects of sin. As earlier discussed, Mother Nature's unpredictable
behaviors are evidence of the curse resulting from the Fall. This
includes global warming, a contentious and often discussed issue
in today's world. The same can be said of volcanic eruptions,
earthquakes, hurricanes, tornadoes, pestilences, and signs in the sun,
moon, and stars.

When the people of Habakkuk's time turned away from God
and began worshipping false idols, God's judgment took the form of
four deadly acts, three of which were acts of nature.

> For this is what the Sovereign Lord says: How much
> worse will it be when I send against Jerusalem my
> four dreadful judgments—sword and famine and
> wild beasts and plague—to kill its men and their
> animals! (Ezekiel 14:21)

Note the judgments: "the sword" or conflict among nations, aberrant behaviors in nature, including droughts, famine, and wild animals behaving badly, and the emergence of deadly viruses and bacteria. Think of the recent COVID epidemic.

These are the very things Jesus indicated will increase in number and severity as sin and wickedness become more prevalent in the days leading up to His return. These all look bleak of course.

However, in describing those difficult days, there is a clear hint of optimism for better days to come. Jesus afforded a surprising and hopeful insight. He compared the aberrant behaviors in nature and the corrupt politics of men to "birth pangs" like what a mother experiences in the final stages of her pregnancy.

> Nation will rise against nation, and kingdom against
> kingdom. There will be famines and earthquakes in
> various places. All these are the beginning of birth
> pains. (Matthew 24:7–8)

These events in nature and the politics of humans sound horrific, but there is hope in Jesus's illustration. Just as the painful contractions a mother experiences in the final stages of her pregnancy lead to the joyous birth of her child, so too the birth pangs the world is currently experiencing are the final stages leading to a glorious rebirth of a new heaven and a new earth. What Jesus did in describing the events leading to this rebirth is like an ultrasound affording us an image of a glorious new world to come.

Had I understood this as a child, the twofold message was evident in the jagged rock formations I had witnessed. Scarred and serrated, the rough-hewn edges of the surrounding mountains and abrupt rock outcroppings rising out of the sea spoke of traumatic past events.

According to the biblical narrative, the evil acts of humans in the early history of humankind had become so deeply entrenched that God in His wrath caused the earth and elements of His universe to become extremely unstable, resulting in the destruction of the first earth. The magnitude of God's judgment against sin is declared by the rugged scenes in nature that surrounded the land where I grew up.

His judgment against sin resulted in the beginnings of a very different earth, one increasingly susceptible to chaos and unpredictability. And ever since, Mother Earth has been gradually experiencing increasing birth pangs while anxiously awaiting the restoration of paradise lost. The anticipation of renewal is not its only message.

In Romans 1:20, we read its most important message. "For since the creation of the world God's invisible qualities—his eternal power and divine nature—have been clearly seen, being understood from what has been made."

So clear is the message creation declares that the apostle Paul concluded, "People are without excuse" when they choose to ignore it.

Therein lies a warning not to misconstrue creation's most important message regarding our Creator.

23

The Farthest Edge
of America

The heavens declare the glory of God; the
skies proclaim the work of his hands. Day
after day they pour forth speech; night
after night they reveal knowledge.
—Psalm 19:1–2

LURED BY THE PRISTINE NATURE OF THE OCEAN AND THE AWE-
inspiring coastline, visitors from every part of the United States and
even distant countries have long made the trek along the winding
two-lane coastal highway to my hometown to experience the beauty
at the far end of America's Olympic Peninsula.

Having served in my community as an elected tribal leader and
pastor of a small church, my wife, Mary, and I would often invite
friends and relatives to join with us in making the trek to Cape
Flattery, the modern name for the "place at the end of the land where
the birds gather."

The short, twenty-minute, downhill hike through a thick forest
of giant cedars, firs, and spruce trees, along with lush ferns lining
the trail, is well worth the effort. Almost immediately, the fresh
smells of the thick forest and the melodic song of forest birds affords
a delightful contrast to the constant noise and glut of traffic so
characteristic of much of urban America.

As we would make our way down the sloping trail toward our destination, the distant sounds of waves surging against the rocky coastline resounded through the forest with increasing resonance the closer we got to the end. Then just as the crescendo of a surging sea reached its peak, a breathtaking seascape suddenly emerged.

From the vantage point of a conveniently placed viewing platform, everywhere were ocean birds of all kinds, including gulls, coots, cormorants, common murres, and puffins, paddling nervously about here and then there, all the while surveying their surroundings for their next meal or wary of becoming one. Joined to the sound of the thunderous surf, their plaintive cries offered a symphony of praise to the One who created everything. You might even catch a glimpse of a whale spouting in the distance.

High above the din of waves crashing on rocky coastline, you might see a sharp-eyed eagle circling about in the thermal troughs. Once it spots its prey, an unfortunate fish that had wandered too near the surface, it swoops down from on high at incredible speed to seize its unsuspecting victim.

With the still squirming fish now firmly secured in its talons, the eagle soars ever upward carrying its protesting victim on a one-way journey to its forest home in the hills, where it will dine in quiet solitude.

Not more than a mile distant, a mostly flat-surfaced island known as Tatoosh resides stone-faced and resolute, a lonely sentinel, hosting an automated lighthouse that through the years has served to warn ships to steer clear of the rock-strewn coastline. Often obscured by fog, this windswept, twelve-acre rock derived its name from an ancient Makah chief.

Affording convenient access to the halibut and salmon fishing "grounds," the island also served as a spring and summer camp for my ancestors, providing easier access to the halibut and salmon that were so abundant.

Captivated by the cape's pristine nature, visitors from all over the United States and some foreign countries typically preserve the scenes I have described in the click of a camera or in the mind as a treasured forever memory.

It is all good of course. Scenes like I have described are provided by our Creator to afford respite from the stresses of life. However, if the good feeling one gets from the natural world becomes a substitute for a genuine appreciation for the God who created everything, then we miss creation's most important message—namely how great our God is.

Unfortunately, this happens far too often in a world that has gradually become distant from God-awe and His righteous laws. Statistics regarding declining church membership clearly reveal this trend away from Him. Naturally when this occurs, people can witness the beauty and magnificence of a scene in nature and miss God altogether. And that is when worship of nature replaces devotion to the One who created it.

The failure to honor the Creator reminds me of our secularized Christmas season where manger scenes no longer appear in front of public schools as they once did and the Christmas tree and Christmas lights no longer symbolize Jesus the light of the world or the cross and His gift of salvation.

The supplanting of creation's ultimate message pointing to our Creator Jesus—"Through him all things were made; without him nothing was made that has been made" (John 1:2)—breeds foolishness.

24

The Way of Fools

The fool says in his heart, "There is no
God." They are corrupt, their deeds are
vile; there is no one who does good.
—Proverbs 14:1

LURED BY THE UNFORGETTABLE VISTAS OF THE NATURAL WORLD
and subjected to modern skepticism, it is easy enough for people
to view a rainbow, a gorgeous sunset, or a majestic mountain scene
and not give glory to the One who created it. The following passage
explains what then can result:

Romans 1:19–21 states,

> For the wrath of God is revealed against all
> ungodliness and wickedness of those who suppress
> the truth. For what can be known about God is plain
> to them. Ever since the creation of the world His
> eternal power and divine nature, invisible though
> they are, have been understood and seen through
> the things He has made.

The apostle Paul further explained what happens to people who
reject God's clear revelation in creation.

> For although they knew God, they neither glorified
> him as God nor gave thanks to him, but their

thinking became futile, and their foolish hearts were darkened. Although they claimed to be wise, they became fools and exchanged the glory of the immortal God for images made to look like a mortal human being and birds and animals and reptiles. (Romans 1:21–23)

This describes what happened to the tribe of Judah during the prophet Habakkuk's time. Having rejected God's revelation in His Word and the testimony of creation, they foolishly reverted to the worship of false gods and forsook their rich history of great leaders of the past who were faithful to God.

This speaks to an issue of vital importance: the need to properly interpret the natural world's declarations concerning our Creator. The apostle Paul concluded that those unwilling to recognize the revelation of our Creator clear in the things He has made are "without excuse" and in their pride and self-reliance "become fools."

The Greek word translated as "fools" is the origin of the English word "moron," an apt description of the person or a nation that fails to reverence the Creator and His righteous laws. That America has increasingly been given to foolishness is suggested by the current state of our nation's affairs. Here is the evidence: despite warnings that increasing the money supply to meet congressional spending goals devalues the dollar and amounts to a tax on the poor because it drives up prices on the necessities. Knowing this, our elected officials have done so anyway. The resulting inflation caused by "too many dollars chasing too few products" makes everything more expensive, especially housing, gas for our cars, and business expansion. In the process, this nation's debt rose from $8 trillion in 2008 and now stands at $34 trillion and growing. Unless we finally hold our leaders more responsible, this nation's foolish fiscal policies will leave our country in a very difficult place for generations to come.

Then there are our nation's open borders. This has resulted in millions of undocumented migrants coming into our country, some with criminal intent, costing our nation billions for education and health care and increasing the possibility of terrorist acts by those enemies of America who slip undetected past our overwhelmed border patrol guards.

This has contributed to a problem I discussed previously: the trafficking of young children for immoral purposes. This is modern-day slavery at its worst. Thousands of children victimized by this horrific practice are emotionally and physically damaged in ways difficult to imagine. And yet our divided congress is paralyzed from taking action to stop such evil. This is not just foolishness; it is evil.

Then there are the illegal drugs like fentanyl smuggled by the Mexican drug cartel across our border. This drug manufactured in China has led to thousands of deaths among our young people. And yet our present leadership refuses to close our borders. By doing nothing to stem the tide, we have invited calamity on this nation's youth as well as opened the door to another dangerous situation, terroristic acts.

Among the millions who have illegally crossed our borders in the last two years are an estimated 20,000 Chinese nationalists, most of whom are said to be of military age. They have simply disappeared into the American landscape. Our government does not know where they are.

Recently, officials in California discovered a clandestine laboratory operated by Chinese nationalists who were conducting lab experiments with the deadly COVID-19 virus. How many labs like this exist throughout America? And who is behind this and for what purpose? And even more troubling, according to a report by Elizabeth Olberding for One America News on September 5, 2023, Chinese nationalists posing as tourists have managed to gain access to over one hundred US military installations with the intention of gathering sensitive data, this according to the FBI and the Department of Defense. The Chinese have also been purchasing land near military bases. Allowing this to happen by a nation that has vowed to replace us as the world's leader is on a scale of foolishness beyond our worst fears.

THE WAY OF FOOLS

What China is doing behind the scenes goes further than even their activities in the US. Victor Davis Hanson, a senior fellow for the Hoover Institute, has reported that in recent years the Chinese have also gained control of fifteen of the major ports of the world that they have been able to lease, rebuild, and refurbish.[7]

Like Habakkuk's concern for his nation, I have wondered why God would allow this avowed atheistic nation that rules its people with fear and aborts millions of its babies to rise to such prominence?

I suspect were God to address my query, He might say something like "Don, I am surprised you would even consider a question like this. You know already that America has foolishly strayed from Me, and while some remain faithful, too many others no longer respect my righteous and eternal laws. And you know too that I am sovereign over all things in creation and the affairs of men, including the rise and fall of nations and their leaders. I will not allow a nation that I have blessed to turn its backs on Me. Why then are you surprised that I have allowed the emergence of the Chinese empire? Or that America is experiencing unprecedented internal difficulties?"

All the above and many other government policies on the environment, energy, unfair application of justice, failure of elected officials to be transparent, and efforts to defund the police reflect foolishness on a scale unprecedented in our nation's history. They are a clear indication that God's providential grace is being withdrawn from our nation and that He is permitting us to be led by fools. To quote the apostle Paul once again, "Professing themselves to be wise, they became fools."

---

[7] *Epoch News*, vol. 52, 5. Number 7/8 July–August 2023.

84

25

The Holy Trinity

*I believe in God the Father Almighty maker of
heaven and earth and Jesus Christ His only
begotten Son who was born of the virgin Mary
and suffered under Pontius Pilate and was
crucified died and buried; and on the third
day he rose again ... and in the Holy Spirit ...*
—The Apostles' Creed

ACKNOWLEDGING OUR CREATOR IS A FIRST STEP IN DELIVERING
our nation from its foolishness. I offer a summary of the historic
nature of the Holy Trinity—God the Father, God the Son, and God
the Holy Spirit—the three Persons of the Godhead, equal in divine
essence and the one true God.

Alarmed by the spread of false teachings concerning the doctrine
of the Holy Trinity, early church fathers convened two special
councils, one in AD 140 from which we got the Apostles' Creed and
a second in AD 325 when the Nicene Creed was developed as a more
complete summary of the Christian faith.

Because it is vital to our Christian faith to honor the Father,
the Son, and the Holy Spirit as One God, Satan, who is a liar and
opposed to God, has attempted to obfuscate the true nature of the
Holy Trinity, especially the Person and work of Jesus.

In the later convened Council of Nicaea in 325, the delegates affirmed the Apostles' Creed but added more detail, summarizing the fundamental teachings of the Christian faith as follows:

> I believe in one God, the Father Almighty, maker of heaven and earth and all things visible and invisible. And in one Lord Jesus Christ, the only begotten Son of God, begotten of his Father before all worlds, God of God, Light of Light, the very God of very God, begotten not made, being of one substance with the Father, by whom all things were made ... and the Holy Spirit as, the Lord and giver of life, who proceeds from the Father and the Son who with the Father and Son together is worshiped and glorified ...

The Athanasian Creed, also written in the 4th century AD, expanded on this further by stating unequivocally:

> "Thus the Father is God; the Son is God; the Holy Spirit is God; and yet there are not three gods, but One God."

No other religion teaches the Triune nature of the Godhead: Father, Son, and Holy Spirit. And none speaks of a Creator God who sent His only Son to give His life on behalf of a fallen human race or speaks of salvation and eternal life freely offered to all those who place their faith and trust in Him.

All of scripture from the Old Testament to the New Testament have these two all-important and primary messages: the centrality of the Triune God in our creation and the truth that from before all eternity God the Father, because of His love for us, determined to send His only begotten Son Jesus into the world to suffer and die on the cross to redeem sinful humankind and to restore paradise lost.

And further, that the Holy Spirit, the Comforter sent by the Father and Son, is the One who reveals Jesus to us.

In 2 Timothy 1:9 we read, "He has saved us and called us to a holy life—not because of anything we have done but because of his own purpose and grace. This grace was given us in Christ Jesus before the beginning of time."

In what is a mystery to us, God already determined to send His Son Jesus to be our Savior and Lord before the beginning of time; His foreknowledge of the Fall into sin and plan to redeem humankind was determined from before the creation of the heavens and the earth. The meaning of your life and mine cannot be understood apart from acknowledging this truth.

What is not a mystery, however, is that none of us can by our own righteousness or deeds merit eternal life. Living a good life, however praiseworthy, does not merit salvation.

Although our human pride may stubbornly insist otherwise, salvation is a freely offered gift of God's grace. Ephesians 2:8–9 affirms,

> For it is by grace you have been saved, through faith—and this is not from yourselves, it is the gift of God—not by works, so that no one can boast.

Our nation's Founding Fathers involved in creating our constitution understood how important it was to devise a constitution firmly based on the principles of the Judeo-Christian values.

They understood too that security can only be assured by trusting in Him. And so came the motto emblazoned on our nation's currency and coins: "In God we trust." And this is the very doctrine that Satan and the Marxist progressives have been attacking and why the Christian faith has been increasingly subject to persecution as our nation drifts further away from Him.

26

The Centrality of Mother Earth

No matter what size ... men may ascribe to
the sun, moon, and stars, their history and
significance are dependent on the earth.
—F. Pieper, *Christian Dogmatics*

BEFORE I CONTINUE MY THEME REGARDING THE CREATION AND
the redemptive act of our Triune God in sending His Son Jesus
to redeem humankind and restore His creation, I want to dispel
a false notion that has increasingly emerged and given rise to the
false assumption that the earth is insignificant in the vastness of the
universe.

According to the Bible, the opposite is true; the earth is unique
and vitally important in the universe, and here is why. Mother Earth is
the place where God chose to create humankind, the place where the
Fall occurred, and the curse originated, and most notably, the location
where Jesus entered our existence to accomplish our salvation. For
that reason, the significance and history of the entire universe is
"dependent on the earth."

Unfortunately, there has been much confusion concerning the
centrality of Mother Earth, partly the result of an error on the part
of the Christian church and partly due to modern science's efforts to
explain the origins of the universe as having evolved over billions of

years. Here is a short history explaining how some came to diminish the earth as central to the universe.

During the Middle Ages, the Roman Catholic Church, following the fall of the Roman Empire around AD 500, had ascended to become the most dominant economic, cultural, and political influence on Europeans. One of the chief teachings of the church as it grew in influence was that the earth was the center of the solar system and the sun and the planets revolved around it.

This idea originally appears to have grown out of the Greek world in the second century AD, with a man named Ptolemy, an early astronomer. His view of the earth as the center and the sun and planets revolving around it eventually became part of the doctrinal teaching of the Roman Catholic Church. While it fit the narrative of earth's importance in God's creation, the teaching was not based on fact.

But then in the sixteenth century, a Polish priest and astronomer, Nicholas Copernicus, advanced the theory released posthumously that the earth and the planets revolved around the sun, a radical departure from church doctrine. Believing his theory to be heresy, the church condemned the idea. It was a contradiction of church doctrine.

Shortly thereafter, Galileo Galilei, following improvements he made to the telescope, confirmed the Copernican view. This too was met with immediate condemnation by church authorities. Galileo was subsequently charged with heresy and ordered to appear before an inquisition, a formal hearing before church officials intended to cause him to repudiate his views.

He was eventually convicted of heresy and forced in 1632 to endure house arrest for ten years, during which time he was forbidden from publishing any of his papers.

By now, the ignorance that shrouded much of the European world including the church began to dissipate as other scientists came along confirming the observations of Copernicus and Galileo. The scientific revolution had begun; a heliocentric (solar) system showing the earth and planets revolving around the sun had been established.

The new era of scientific discovery with its focus on observation and testing to arrive at truth, while a welcome departure from the ignorance of previous generations, began to erode confidence in the biblical explanation for our origins.

This set the stage for the elevation of science over the Bible. Long periods of time and the theory of evolution soon supplanted a biblical explanation.

With God increasingly pushed to the periphery, science emerged as a means of solving all of humankind's ills and providing all the answers relative to the meaning of our existence. This new era of scientific discovery came to be known as the Age of Enlightenment and the Age of Reason. Secular humanism rose to prominence; European man and his genius could solve all our problems. In 1875, William Ernest Henley captured the essence of the Age of Reason in his poem "Invictus." "It matters not how strait the gait, how charged the punishments ... I am the master of my fate. I am the captain of my soul."

Ever since the scientific revolution began and humankind's reason was elevated, there has continued to be an ongoing debate regarding the age of the universe, how it formed, and whether a Creator God exists. This discussion has through the years gradually led to another misconception. There is life on other planets and aliens are regularly visiting our planet in advanced spacecraft. Some who are convinced of this hope these alleged beings have our best interests in mind and can save us from self-destruction.

None of this is true, and I will explain why.

27

The Alien Deception

MODERN SCIENTIFIC THEORY ADVANCED IN PUBLIC SCHOOLS AND universities estimates the age of the universe to be 13.7 billion years old when they have theorized a great explosion occurred that began creation. Or at least that is what they used to believe. Now scientists, since the advent of the James Webb Space Telescope, have changed even that number to a far more distant time.

In all their calculations, they have concluded that the earth is not the center of the universe. And having endorsed evolution and eons of time, they have posed the further theory that given its massive dimensions, other intelligent life-forms surely had to have evolved.

And further, some very credible people believe beings from distant planets make regular visits to earth. The upswing in sightings of UFOs in recent years has only reinforced this idea and led many to speculate about their origin and what they are doing.

As you may be aware, there has been a long-standing conspiracy theory that the US government is in possession of the remains of aliens killed in the Nevada desert where their space craft is alleged to have crashed and that they have been deliberately concealing the information from the public. My point in countering these speculations is this: The idea of other worlds inhabited by aliens is not supported in the Bible. And while our Creator certainly could have created other life-forms on other planets if He willed, scripture makes no mention of their existence except those other worldly beings that exist in the presence of God in heaven. Among these are angels, cherubim, seraphim, and the beings that continually surround the throne of God.

And of course, there are Satan and the fallen angels (demons) who were cast out of heaven because of their rebellion against God.

These devils exist in our world today and often appear in grotesque forms and even as angels of light. Mostly, however, they remain hidden from view, except in certain situations where a house is haunted (as in the house where I lived) or someone describes having seen strange manifestations that, in their appearance, look to me more like demons.

So what accounts for the many sightings of unidentified flying objects? Are they Chinese spy balloons? Advanced military planes we know nothing about? Signs from God or space debris from the thousands of satellites circling our planet, or simply wayward weather balloons? Maybe all the above.

Or could some of these sightings be demonic in origin intended to distract people from the truth that the earth is the center of the vast universe, the location where the curse wrought by sin originated, and the place where Jesus, the Son of God, came to suffer and die on the cross to save the human race and ultimately to restore the earth and universe from the curse of the Fall?

Satan, the master of deception and disguise, and capable of masking his intentions as the "father of lies," has always attempted, as I pointed out, to obfuscate the true nature of Jesus's Person and work. Getting humans into endless speculations about alien life-forms from distant galaxies is one of the ways I believe he does this.

It seems very plausible for me to conclude therefore that some of the strange manifestations people are witnessing in the skies above or even grotesque creatures of unknown species appearing in the wild are satanic in origin.

Once again, my point is to underline the truth that the focus of God and His salvation plan for humankind is and always has been centered on humankind and the earth, not the universe. In truth, as

I have related, the universe was cursed by the Fall and looks forward to the day when it too will be transformed on the day Jesus returns.

Knowing this, we should not allow ourselves to be seduced into endless speculations about other beings from other worlds and their intentions. Aside from Satan and his demon hordes, aliens from other worlds do not exist.

As is affirmed in John 3:16, "For God so loved the world that he gave his one and only Son, that whoever believes in him shall not perish but have eternal life." Nowhere does this verse imply that Jesus died to save other beings on planets far away. Believing in other worldly visitors is a distraction from the true message that God "so loved the world" that He sent His Son Jesus into this world to save humankind from the curse of sin and by extension the entire universe.

In Psalm 19:1, we read, "The heavens declare the glory of God; the skies proclaim the work of his hands."

And therefore, I can assure my reader that, as massive as the universe is, Mother Earth, where humankind dwells and where Jesus entered our existence, is central to all of God's creation.

The unbelievable expanse of the universe is telling us something very important about our Creator we need to know. He is incredibly, *mind-boggedly* bigger than we can imagine. And realizing this should comfort us in all of our trials and tribulations in this world.

28

Space Is Big; God Is Bigger

Space is big. Really big. You won't believe
how vastly hugely mind-boggedly big it is.
—Douglas Adams, *Hitchhiker's Guide to the Galaxy*

IN HIS COMIC ALLEGORY *A HITCHHIKER'S GUIDE TO THE GALAXY*, author Douglas Adams explains how his main character, Arthur Dent, is suddenly plucked off the earth by aliens just before they destroy it to make way for a "hyperspatial express route," a kind of galactic freeway for alien transport.

Earthlings should have known this would occur and protested during the comment period, but even if they knew of such a hearing (which they didn't) earthlings did not have the means to travel to a distant part of the galaxy.

After all, as one of the books main characters states, "Space is big. Really big. You just won't believe how vastly hugely mind-boggedly big it is. I mean you may think it is a long way down the road to the chemist, but that is just peanuts to space …"[8]

Adams in real life was an atheist. Nevertheless, he captured the obvious: the universe is incredibly, "mind-boggedly big." He just didn't get the message that its immense dimensions and complexity were proof that God existed.

To give you a sense of the immense dimensions of the universe and the immeasurable power and creative genius it attests to our

---

[8] Adams, Douglas. *The Hitchhiker's Guide to the Galaxy*. Random House, 1980.

Creator, scientists have estimated that the universe contains at least 2 trillion galaxies, each containing billions upon billions of stars. That number keeps going up as they learn more.

The ever-changing estimates are due in part to the far-reaching capabilities afforded by the Hubble Space Telescope and more recently the James Webb Space Telescope. Based in part on their far-reaching capabilities, scientists have calculated that if all the stars in all the galaxies of the universe were added together, their total would exceed all the grains of sand on all the shores of the entire earth!

My mother surely could have appreciated this. She was a meticulous housekeeper—everything in its place and her linoleum floors kept spotless. Managing what she could control was I suspect her way of dealing with the chaos surrounding her life. Now imagine this scene: After a day of rollicking fun on the beach, much to my mother's consternation, I would return home only to track countless grains of sand in my shoes and pockets onto her meticulously maintained floor. Determined to maintain order, she would accost me at the entrance to her home and demand that I immediately take off my shoes, socks, and pants and empty their contents. At least a couple of tablespoons worth of sand in my shoes, socks, pockets, and even my hair would be shaken out.

Amazingly, there are people who have taken a heaping teaspoon of sand and painstakingly counted each individual grain. It amounts to about 80,000 to 100,000 per teaspoon. That depends on whether you are counting sand taken from the West Coast of the US (larger in size) or the Gulf of Mexico (smaller). Grains of sand vary in size.

I estimate the number of individual grains of sand I typically would track into my mother's home (about 400,000) is an incomprehensibly tiny representation of the total of all the grains of sand on all the beaches of the world. And then imagine this recent calculation: for every grain of sand on all the beaches of the world, there are said to be 10,000 stars.

And what is more astounding, according to Psalm 147:4, is our Creator "determines the number of the stars and calls them each by name."

And further, each one of these stars in all the galaxies in the vast universe offers praise to Him. Psalm 148:3–4 reads,

> Praise him, sun and moon; praise him, all you shining stars. Praise him, you highest heavens and you waters above the skies.

Caught up in our often skeptical, science-driven world, we might be tempted to believe this could not possibly be true. How is it possible that trillions upon trillions of these massive stars whose numbers exceed all the grains of sand on all the beaches on the earth offer praise to their Creator? Is this just a figure of speech?

In researching for my book, I came across the discovery of an interesting phenomenon made possible by powerful radio telescopes able for the first time to probe deep into space and capable of listening to the electromagnetic impulses that are unique to each star. This relatively new technology enabling scientists to listen in on these impulses has led to a new classification in astronomy known as asteroseismology.

While you and I cannot hear the sounds stars make since space is a virtual vacuum, the electromagnetic pulses they give off have enabled astrophysicists to discern something fascinating. The biggest stars are said to make the lowest sounds and smaller stars make high-pitched sounds like a flute. Aggregated, they resonate like a symphony in outer space. I would submit that this is a symphony choreographed for our Creator by these celestial bodies.

It is evidence, if you can accept this by faith, that our Creator's engagement with things incredibly large and infinitely small is far beyond our capacity to comprehend.

This sheds a light on what Jesus said to his Pharisee and Sadducee critics angry that a vast throng of people were praising Him as He made His triumphal entry into Jerusalem on the first Palm Sunday.

Along the way into Jerusalem, vast numbers of people lined the street and proclaimed, "Hosanna to the highest, blessed is he that comes in the name of the Lord."

This did not go over well with Jesus's critics. The Sadducees and Pharisees, jealous of His fame and angry that He claimed to be the Messiah, demanded He tell the vast throng lining the street to stop. Jesus responded to their criticism, "I tell you ... if they keep silent, the stones will cry out" (Luke 19:40).

What? Two trillion galaxies and trillions upon trillions of stars within them praise Him. And the rocks too? It seems absurd. However, everything Jesus has made, whether the subatomic particles that make up everything in the universe and the rocks we so easily dismiss as inanimate or the massive stars in the heavens above, all things big and small, are held together by Him and, upon His command, do His bidding. His engagement with things big and small, even the trees that "clap their hands" in praise of Him or the lilies of the fields that He daily clothes or the care He has for every bird that falls to the ground—all testify to His intimate engagement with His creation.

Colossians 1:15–17 says this about Jesus:

> The Son is the image of the invisible God, the firstborn over all creation. For in him all things were created: things in heaven and on earth, visible and invisible, whether thrones or powers or rulers or authorities; all things have been created through him and for him. He is before all things, and in him all things hold together.

Take Jesus out of the equation of sustaining the universe moment by moment and all things big or small would instantly fly apart. And the universe knows He is the Creator and Sustainer of all things and in response sing His praises.

And so, it should not surprise us that Jesus was able to take five loaves of bread and two fish and feed five thousand men along with an additional number of women and children and have twelve baskets of food left over. And then when the disciples got into a boat to cross the Sea of Galilee and the winds and seas threatened to sink their boat, Jesus had only to command the wind and waves to cease, and they immediately obeyed Him.

So stunned and in awe of Jesus's command over nature that His disciples confessed, "Truly you are the Son of God" (Matthew 14:33). All creation obeys His will.

The incredible nature of our God who created the vast universe with countless stars and planets is welcome news for us, especially in a world growing increasingly more dangerous and as we individually face difficult personal challenges. No matter how hopeless things may appear in our world or in our lives, our Creator God reigns supreme over everything. And He can meet our every need no matter how difficult things in life may seem. *Why do we even doubt?*

In the following chapters, I will focus on four major eras of Mother Earth. These eras in Mother Earth's history affords a clue to what our all-powerful God is doing and will do in the future. Mother Earth and the entire universe always do His bidding, and this can be made evident to us.

29

The First Era of Mother Earth

In the beginning God created the heavens and
the earth. Now the earth was formless and empty,
darkness was over the surface of the deep, and
the Spirit of God was hovering over the waters.
—Genesis 1:1

BECAUSE THIS IS A SUMMARY AND NOT A COMMENTARY ON THE
full narrative in Genesis, I will address only the key elements leading
to my theory that there have been four very distinct eras in the history
of Mother Earth, with a fifth one yet to come. I begin with the First
Era of Mother Earth.

In the beginning when God created the earth, it was dark,
disordered, and chaotic, "a formless void." In scientific terms, the
evident disorganization of the earth would be characterized as "high
entropy" or disordered.

Then according to Genesis, this sequence occurred to organize
the chaos. On day 1, God created the earth, space, and time. On day
2, He created the atmosphere, firmament, and the expanse. On day
3, He made dry land and plants. On day 4, He created the sun, the
moon, and the stars. On day 5, He made the sea and flying creatures.
And on day 6, He made land animals and man—the best saved for
last. Then on the seventh day, He rested from all that He had created.

In Genesis 1:25, we read God's assessment of His creative works. "God saw that it was good."

Then in Genesis 1:26–27, we read,

> Then God said, "Let us make mankind in our image, in our likeness ... So God created mankind in His own image, in the image of God He created them."

Created in His image sets humankind above all other of God's creation. That does not mean to imply, however, that we are like Him in His eternal power and glory. There is no need for pride here. To the contrary, we are infinitely small by comparison to Him.

Our Creator placed Adam and his helpmeet, Eve, in the middle of a wondrous garden He called "Eden," a name that meant "delight."

Eden and the perfect world surrounding the Garden was the First Era of Mother Earth and Adam and Eve, the first humans charged to care for it.

Imagine their world. Beautiful surroundings, wondrous birds, and animals unafraid of them, coupled with great sunrises and sunsets and all the food they needed or desired.

Blessed with a uniformly tropical climate, this paradise seems to have been watered with a gentle mist that rose from the surrounding lands to irrigate the lush plant life.

Another characteristic different from our present era is that the earth was a single landmass surrounded by vast seas. By way of contrast, today there are seven continents and numerous islands formed by volcanoes scattered here and there.

The vast universe I described also had to have been far different. It was designed to sustain life on earth, not destroy it.

Today we face numerous threats from outer space like the deadly rays that contribute to aging, asteroids that could annihilate life on earth, or exploding stars producing deadly gamma rays and black holes, the remnants of exploded stars, that could, if we got close enough, suck our earth into oblivion.

Even the sun that provides us with light and warmth, enabling life on planet Earth, poses a grave danger to us were it to suddenly release massive amounts of solar energy known as a coronal mass ejection (CME) as occurred in 1859.

The radiation from the sun at that time fried all the electrical lines, obliterating the means of communication all over the world. This at a time when electrical power was in its infancy and people were not dependent on an electrical grid as we are today. Thus, the effects were minimal.

However, it is not hard to imagine that, were a similar coronal ejection to occur today as some scientists think could happen, it would destroy our nation's power grid, prevent cars from being able to start, disable computers, cell phones and anything requiring electricity. Our cities would go dark.

The resulting chaos from an event like this would pit people against each other in a desperate effort to find food and water. It would take years for the survivors to recover. But that is the reality of our world.

By way of contrast, the perfect universe God created in the beginning was designed to preserve life on earth, not destroy it.

Clearly the First Era of Mother Earth was a paradise on a scale none of us can fully imagine—a safe environment where things did not wear out, rust out, fall apart, or die and animals did not prey on one another. A place where Murphy's law—everything that can go wrong will go wrong at the worst possible moment—did not apply and where chaos and unpredictability in weather patterns did not occur. Every day in Eden was a delightful experience. This is ultimately the paradise God intended for us.

A place where

> the sound of weeping and of crying will be heard in it no more. Never again will there be in it an infant who lives but a few days, or an old man who does not live out his years; the one who dies at a hundred

will be thought a mere child; the one who fails to reach a hundred will be considered accursed. They will build houses and dwell in them; they will plant vineyards and eat their fruit. No longer will they build houses and others live in them, or plant and others eat. For as the days of a tree, so will be the days of my people; my chosen ones will long enjoy the work of their hands. They will not labor in vain, nor will they bear children doomed to misfortune; for they will be a people blessed by the Lord, they, and their descendants with them. Before they call, I will answer; while they are still speaking, I will hear.

The wolf and the lamb will feed together, and the lion will eat straw like the ox. (Isaiah 65:19–25)

In other words, the First Era of Mother Earth was a paradise unlike anything we have experienced, a wondrous place where order and harmony were the way of life and intimate conversation with a loving God as natural as you might have with your loved ones. Quite simply, Eden was a place, whether we are aware of it or not, that we all long to experience.

And so, what could possibly go wrong? We know of course that something did. Our first parents in defiance of the will of God ate of the tree of the knowledge of good and evil, resulting in death and corruption to humankind and all creation.

Had Adam and Eve determined to obey our Creator and not eaten of the forbidden fruit, the wondrous world of uniformly comfortable weather, gorgeous sunrises and sunsets, lovely palms and flowers of all kinds, and animals and birds that were unafraid of humans would be the only era of Mother Earth we would know.

And more importantly, we would know and experience that God loves us, and we would love Him and our neighbor. And no one would get old and die, and our children would not suffer calamity.

Unfortunately, sin has corrupted everything, ushering in a world where man and beast, the earth and universe, have been subject to mortality and things get sick and die. A world where we often feel alone and we don't belong. Much like homeless people surely must feel. A world where perfect order was now subject to disorder and things could deteriorate and fall apart.

I call the introduction of this sad new reality the Second Era of Mother Earth.

30

The Second Era of Mother Earth

The Lord God made all kinds of trees grow
out of the ground—trees that were pleasing
to the eye and good for food. In the middle
of the garden were the tree of life and the
tree of the knowledge of good and evil.
—Genesis 2:9

THERE WAS ANOTHER TREE IN THE GARDEN OF EDEN, "THE TREE of Life." It is evidence of God's grace that Adam and Eve were prevented from eating of the fruit of that tree.

Had they eaten of the fruit of the fruit of the Tree of Life, generations of humans to follow would forever be condemned to eternal death without the possibility of redemption. In Genesis 3:24, we read that therefore God "drove the man out, he placed on the east side of the Garden of Eden cherubim and a flaming sword flashing back and forth to guard the way to the tree of life."

In what I have labeled the Second Era of Mother Earth, children born to Adam and Eve and all succeeding generations were conceived in sin. The psalmist acknowledged this reality when he wrote, "Behold, I was shaped in iniquity and in sin did my mother conceive me." And later the apostle Paul wrote in Romans 3:23, "For all have sinned and fall short of the glory of God."

The first evidence of the way sin impacted our first parents was the shame and guilt they felt after disobeying the Creator. Aware of their nakedness for the first time, they felt guilt and shame and were afraid of God. They tried to hide their sin by covering their nakedness and making excuses for their wrongdoing. Adam blamed God for giving him Eve; she in turn blamed the serpent.

It was the first instance where humans were unwilling to take responsibility for their sinful behavior. Lying and rationalization were introduced into the human experience. Consider how often this sin is manifest in our culture today, especially by some of our political leaders interested more in maintaining their power and status than telling the truth.

It appears the passage of time must have changed too. Mother Nature and all creation began to show age and mortality; things could wear out and everything began to die, especially the people God had intended would live forever.

Entropy, a process that describes how things in a system like the universe, our bodies, or even something as simple as a melting ice cube on a plate goes from order (low entropy) to high entropy (disorder) when it melts into a puddle of water.

In its state of mortality, Mother Earth began to manifest unpredictable and sometimes destructive behaviors. Crops could now fail, thorns and thistles could invade the garden, accidents could happen, and fish populations could suddenly disappear, and if anything could go wrong, it would at the worst possible moment.

Life in the post-Eden world had become a struggle. Even more problematic, evil began to spread. Increasing idolatry, violence, vengeance, greed, immorality, child sacrifice, war, lust for power, and prejudices of all kinds are just some of the behaviors that began to characterize the world after the Fall.

Eventually evil became so prevalent and the pursuit of pleasures so widespread that there were few God-fearing people left.

However, one man is a noteworthy exception. His name was Enoch, son of Jared, who is described in Genesis 5:22 as a man who "walked faithfully with God." This brief introduction suggests that he surely loved the Lord God with his whole heart, soul, and mind and that he grieved with great sadness a world of people increasingly wicked and determined to rebel against God.

Because of this, it appears God decided to spare Enoch from having to witness the coming judgment. Genesis 5:24 says of Enoch, "Then he was no more, because God took him away ..." It means Enoch never suffered physical death but was translated directly into God's presence. Only one other person in biblical history, the prophet Elijah, was taken in similar fashion.

Under the curse of the Fall, the natural world sensed the immoral behavior of humans and their rejection of the Creator.

We see evidence of this in Genesis 4:10 when the first murder took place. After Cain killed his brother, Abel, God said to him, "Your brother's blood cries out to me from the ground." The earth sensed the evil act and declared it to God. The murder of Abel was the beginning of many sorrows as immorality, murder, greed, pride, and lust for power began to proliferate and dominate human existence.

Although clearly not what it had been before the Fall, it appears that the Second Era of Mother Earth retained some of the life-extending characteristics of the First Era and remained in many ways a kind of paradise.

Gorgeous scenes were everywhere, and the single landmass surrounded by a vast ocean and adorned with pristine lakes and lovely mountains appears to have enjoyed a uniformly tropical climate, just as the First Era of Mother Earth.

While the Second Era no longer experienced the benefits of a universe that preserved life, conditions were still favorable enough for the people of that time to live far longer than people do today. Methuselah, the most famous of these and the son of Enoch, lived to be 969 years old.

Apparently plant life too continued to flourish everywhere and large creatures like dinosaurs apparently thrived on the abundance of leafy trees and plants of all kinds. With the abundance of readily available foods, these large animals were not yet given to prey on humankind or the many varieties of animals that God had created.

I suspect too that Mother Earth was less likely to experience horrific events in nature like the violent storms, earthquakes, and volcanoes we see occurring in our world today.

This was due in part to the likelihood that the earth had not yet experienced the violent disruptions leading to the formation of plate tectonics that would eventually result from the traumas the earth was about to undergo during the cataclysmic events of the Great Flood. However, all that was good about the Second Era of Mother Earth was about to dramatically change. And that is because the spread of evil had reached a tipping point with God. In Genesis 6:5, we read this sad commentary: "The Lord saw how great the wickedness of the human race had become on the earth, and that every inclination of the thoughts of the human heart was only evil all the time."

We should not take this lightly. It reveals that humankind is by nature at war with God.

What may have contributed to the growing rebellion against God during the Second Era of Mother Earth were some unusual beings known as the Nephilim. They are not like us. They appear to have possessed skills and talents that set them apart from the rest of humanity.

31

The Nephilim

> The Nephilim were on the earth in those days—and
> also afterward—when the sons of God went into the
> daughters of humans, who bore children to them.
> —Genesis 6:4

IN THE BOOK OF GENESIS ARE REFERENCES TO "OTHER WORLDLY"
beings referred to as "the sons of God." They were not aliens from
another planet. Whoever they were, most likely angelic beings gone
bad (demons), they were able to take wives from the daughters of men
and produce offspring that were superior to humans.

In Genesis 6:1–2 we read of their origins.

> When human beings began to increase in number
> on the earth and daughters were born to them,
> the sons of God saw that the daughters of humans
> were beautiful, and they married any of them they
> chose.

From this strange union came unusual offspring, the Nephilim.

This hybrid mix appears to have been imposing in physical size
as well as possessing superior knowledge. I can't help but wonder the
pain the daughters of ordinary humans must have experienced while
giving birth to these unusual offspring. I wonder too whether they
were forced to cohabit with these otherworldly beings "who took
wives of all that they chose."

In the book of Enoch, a narrative not recognized as part of the biblical canon, these "sons of God" were originally sent to earth to watch over humans. Instead, they lusted after the comely daughters of men, producing offspring who possessed advanced knowledge and were giants. Whether this is an accurate picture, we cannot know since the narrative falls outside biblical revelation. Nevertheless, Genesis 6:4 affords us a hint of their unique capabilities when it says "these were the heroes that were of old, warriors of renown."

In the context, it may not be so much a compliment as it is a tribute to their extraordinary physical and technical prowess. Could these impressive beings be responsible for the construction of the advanced stone buildings or megaliths found throughout the world and that seem to predate the post-Flood advanced civilizations of the Middle East?

These ancient structures, the remains of ancient civilizations, appear to have used advanced building techniques to construct temples, aqueducts, courtyards, and ornate pillars that rival anything the Greeks and Romans would later build. What is even more impressive is some of the massive stone structures are made of granite weighing hundreds of tons. How did they move these stones blocks from distant quarries without powerful bulldozers and other machinery? And what tools did they use to fashion them with such precision? No one knows.

Evidence for these ancient ruins is found in many places, including Egypt, Turkey, Iraq, Iran, England, Africa, Southeast Asia, South America, and North America.

Among the most well-known are the pyramids in ancient Egypt, especially the Great Pyramid of Giza. While modern archaeologists generally credit Egyptian artisans employing a vast army of laborers utilizing primitive tools like hammers and chisels to construct the Great Pyramid of Giza, it stretches the imagination to understand how this was feasible given the dimensions and engineering techniques required that included the transport of an estimated 2.4 million stone blocks, each weighing 2.5 tons, all cut to precision so that they fit together perfectly to form the pyramid. The nearby Sphinx presents similar mysteries concerning its construction as well as its origins.

In the Americas, one of the more intriguing stone structures, besides Machu Pichu in Peru or the great structures of the Maya civilization, is the megaliths of Tiahuanaco and Puma Punku located high in the Andes of Bolivia, near Lake Titicaca. Said by some to have been constructed by an unknown people as many as 15,000 years ago, Eric von Daniken, author of the best-selling book *Chariots of The Gods*, was so impressed with the site that he proposed a novel idea: that aliens from other worlds were responsible.

What he and others observed were perfectly formed H-blocks weighing many tons joined with other crafted blocks of granite that fit together so perfectly that it was impossible to slip a piece of paper between them. Perfectly bored holes in some of the granite blocks suggested advanced drilling techniques requiring hardened drill bits thought to be unknown to primitive cultures.

So impressed were the Spanish conquistadors with Puma Punku that they took the Inca ruler to the ancient site. When they asked him who was responsible for the impressive structures, the Inca ruler denied his people had anything to do with it. Instead, he credited their ancient god, Viracocha, the Andean creator and "destroyer of the worlds," the father of all Inca gods and the creator of all living things, including the sun, moon, and the stars.

According to their mythology, Viracocha created out of stone a superior race of giants; they were responsible for the construction of the incredible stone megaliths. And just as the Genesis narrative appears to suggest, these beings were unruly and evil, so much so that Viracocha was forced to destroy them with a great flood. Then out of clay, Viracocha created a new race of humans to repopulate the earth.

You can see the similarity to the Genesis narrative. Giants are created; they are possessed of great strength and skills. But they are evil and unruly. They are destroyed by a great flood and a new race of humans emerges.

In the context of the introduction of the Nephilim in Genesis 6, it seems that shortly after their appearance, evil proliferated more widely than before throughout the earth. Did these hybrid half human beings accelerate sin in the world?

From the context, I suspect they did. What happened shortly after the introduction of the Nephilim was the world of the Second Era of Mother Earth became so corrupt and evil that our Creator God

> regretted that he had made human beings on the earth, and his heart was deeply troubled. So, the Lord said, "I will wipe from the face of the earth the human race I have created." (Genesis 6:6–7)

What a tragic commentary on human nature corrupted by sin. This should serve as a warning to America and the world. There is a time when the cup of God's wrath is filled and a tipping point is reached. Consider the progression.

Surrounded by a wondrous creation and talented in mind as well as body and possessing amazing technological skills, the people allowed their pride and sinful passions to take over. They quickly forgot God and His goodness. We can imagine that this was accompanied by rampant immorality on a scale we have not seen.

In their suicidal pact with evil, people turned more and more to the idolatrous worship of the sun and animals and likely practiced child sacrifice, an evil practice that always seems to accompany idolatry wherever and whenever it raises its ugly head.

It was for this reason that God repented that He had made humans. This led to the Third Era of Mother Earth, an incredible remake of planet Earth preceded by a Great Flood—an event so devastating and widespread that it resulted in the death of all humankind including, the animals and even the giants, although in what is a mystery, their descendants reappear in the post-Flood world.

Thankfully, there was one man who remained faithful to God during this evil generation: the man Noah who, along with his family, was saved from the deluge on board a large vessel called the ark.

To accomplish the wholesale destruction of the Second Era of Mother Earth, our Creator chose to use the very creation He had made, including the release of subterranean waters, asteroids striking the earth, earthquakes, volcanoes, tsunamis, powerful storms, and forty days and nights of incessant downpours. It is a reminder that when God calls on His creation to serve His purposes, especially His wrath, no amount of conservation or environmental precautions will prevent the inevitable.

The result is the Third Era of Mother Earth: a world and a universe vastly different from what had been.

32

The Third Era of Mother Earth

The Lord then said to Noah, "Go into the ark,
you and your whole family, because I have
found you righteous in this generation."
—Genesis 7:1

INTENT ON PRESERVING HIS PLAN FOR THE SALVATION OF humankind, God's primary intent all along, God told Noah, a God-fearing man, to build an ark because He was going to destroy the world with a great flood. Genesis 6:8 says volumes about Noah's character. "But Noah found favor in the eyes of the Lord."

A grandson of Methuselah and a righteous man in a sin-obsessed world, Noah began constructing a giant wood boat. You can imagine the degree of faith required to attempt such a project.

People surely had to have thought of him a fool. After all, who in their right mind constructs a giant boat in the middle of paradise when everything including the weather is so pleasant—and then dares to tell people "God has decided to destroy the world"?

Naturally no one likes to hear of coming judgments, especially when they have plans for the good life and are caught up in the sinful pleasures of the world. People in those days were thinking about marriage, having children, growing their investments, and spending time enjoying life in this world.

There is a warning in this. Jesus said,

> As it was in the days of Noah, so it will be at the
> coming of the Son of Man. For in the days before the
> flood, people were eating and drinking, marrying,
> and giving in marriage, up to the day Noah entered
> the ark. (Matthew 24:37–38)

Imagine what Noah's immediate family must have thought when he told them that God had commanded him to build a giant boat far from the sea and in the middle of some field. I can imagine his children saying, "Father, are you out of your mind? Are you sure God told you to do this?" The discussion at the dinner table in that family must have been strained at times.

Still, Noah, a man of great faith, ignored the noise and persevered with the planning, design, acquisition of materials, organization, and hiring of labor to begin the construction.

After 120 years constructing the ark in the face of constant derision on the part of onlookers and maybe even dissension and doubt among members of his family, the ark was finally completed. What a momentous moment that had to have been when the last nail was driven, the compartments for the variety of animals were completed and food and supplies were loaded.

The 120-year construction period suggests graciousness on the part of God. The locals likely thought it was evidence that Noah was a fool. In their blindness, they failed to properly interpret the signs afforded by the progress toward the ark's construction. Every timber added, every nail pounded, and every year that passed was a sign of coming judgment.

In 2 Peter 3:9, the apostle Peter, in describing the time between this present age and the coming judgment of our world, wrote, "The Lord is not slow in keeping his promise, as some understand slowness. Instead, He is patient with you, not wanting anyone to perish, but everyone to come to repentance." This question seems applicable.

If people would have listened to Noah and repented of their evil ways, would God have changed His mind about destroying their world? I suspect He would have.

Apparently none of the people took Noah seriously so we don't know. I also suspect, as the time of completion drew near, the natural world too must have begun to send ominous warning signals not unlike some of the things we are witnessing in nature today.

These likely would have included the creature world. Sensing imminent danger, God's animals must have begun to behave in strange ways.

Chaotic behavior in horses, cows, sheep, birds, dogs, elephants, and even porpoises often occur as much as twenty hours before a major earthquake is about to take place. How they seem to know something is about to happen is more mystery than proven science, although some suggest that they can sense electrical impulses emanating from deep underground that often precede earthquakes.

With the building of the ark completed, the Creator then directed Noah, his family, and a select number of animals needed to repopulate the earth to enter the ark. These animals, apparently anticipating the coming cataclysm, were compliant and cooperative.

With his family and all the animals safely on the vessel and the day of judgment imminent, clouds began to form on the horizon, the wind began to pick up, and the skies became increasingly dark, much to the surprise of the people. This was likely accompanied by powerful earthquakes as the earth itself was subject to powerful forces. Fear and terror and an overwhelming desire to flee to safety surely had to have overtaken the entire population. The people had ignored Noah for 120 years. And now it was too late.

With the earth subject to incredible internal stresses, it is likely that strange sounds from somewhere deep within the earth began to reverberate throughout the land as the plates began to shift and collide. Birds surely would have taken to the air and fled in panic while land animals began rushing toward the hills to find higher ground.

Then at precisely the right moment, God's creation, in obedience to His command, unleashed unprecedented violence upon the world. Powerful rainstorms inundated cities with floodwaters, asteroids began to slam the earth, and violent shaking of the entire earth could be felt as fissures within the depths of the earth began to erupt, releasing incredible amounts of subterranean water.

So massive and powerful was the assault on Mother Earth that upheavals of rock pushed mountains to unprecedented heights; the tilt of the earth may also have been altered.

Lush plants that proliferated everywhere on earth were suddenly subjected to massive upheaval, the crush so great that coal and oil deposits were formed out of the debris of plants and animals. Oil, a key component of our energy, is called "a fossil fuel," the remains of these ancient plants and animals.

Mother Earth was undergoing massive transformation, not over billions of years as modern evolution theorists count time but moment by moment as powerful forces were unleashed.

And with these stresses came another major change: the upper crust of Mother Earth, now fractured, resulted in what today is known as plate tectonics, the scientific theory that the earth's lithosphere comprises a number of large tectonic plates that are always on the move, sometimes resulting in earthquakes.

During the horrendous tumult, the earth's upper mantle was drastically altered. Mother Earth was now increasingly susceptible to volcanic eruptions and earthquakes as the platelets that form the earth's upper crust began moving in opposing directions, sometimes colliding against and under (subducting) or building increasing stresses as one plate moved in the opposite direction of another. It wasn't just the earth that was undergoing dramatic change.

The universe too, including the galaxies and planets, also appears to have been dramatically altered. Everything God made was subject to mortality.

So dramatic were the forces for change that from that time forward, the earth and the entire universe became increasingly subject to unpredictability and chaos. And that included the threat of asteroids and meteors colliding with the earth, sudden releases of the sun's energy (coronal mass ejection), black holes, etc. And more immediate, conditions on earth now allowed for powerful storms to develop, such as hurricanes and other weather phenomena.

This combination of creation gone berserk killed every living thing on the face of the earth, including the great dinosaurs whose remains are often found in Wyoming, South Dakota, and Montana grouped together on hillsides along with many other animals, as if desperate to escape floodwaters, which they were.

The Nephilim perished as well in the carnage, but because they appear part demon in origin, something about their spiritual and physical DNA seems to have survived to reappear in the post-Flood world. I wonder if something of their DNA still exists today but takes on different manifestations.

We do know they were still around post-Flood because of the report many years later by spies sent by Moses to assess the land of Canaan. Upon returning from their mission, the spies reported encountering the Anakites, giant offspring of Anak. "We saw the Nephilim there ... We seemed like grasshoppers in our own eyes, and we looked the same to them" (Numbers 13:33).

Later David, eventual king of Israel, encountered and killed Goliath. This may have ended the physical aspect of this ancient union of "the sons of God and daughters of men," but is it possible the spirit of the demonic component could still exist in our world today? If so, what kind of mischief could these evil beings be responsible for today?

Looking back to my childhood, the majestic rock formations that frame the Olympic National Park near my homeland and the evidence of volcanic rock scattered here and there along the beaches testify to the dynamic traumas that changed Mother Earth.

Not only was the geography radically different from what had been, but the people of the post-Flood earth did not live as long as the people of the previous world.

Peculiar behaviors in nature also began to manifest. What science identifies as chaos theory seemed to apply; it is the idea that a tiny, barely perceptible occurrence in nature, under the right environmental conditions, can morph into something of far greater magnitude.

33

Chaos Theory

Where chaos begins, classical science stops. For
as long as the world has had physicists inquiring
into the laws of nature, it has suffered a special
ignorance about disorder in the atmosphere,
in the turbulent sea, in the fluctuations of
wildlife populations, in the oscillation of the
heart and brain. The irregular side of nature, the
discontinuous and erratic side—these have been
puzzles to science, or worse, monstrosities.
—James Gleick, *Chaos*

ACCORDING TO CHAOS THEORY, AND ITS RELATED ILLUSTRATION
the butterfly effect, a barely noticeable disturbance in the atmosphere
caused by a butterfly flapping its wings off the coast of Africa could,
according to the theory, under the right environmental conditions,
morph into a major hurricane. It is almost always unpredictable
and erratic in its formation, even though we generally know certain
atmospheric conditions and ocean temperatures contribute to their
formation.

Edward Lorenz, a meteorologist/mathematician, is generally
credited for recognizing this phenomenon. In 1961, to find a way to
accurately forecast weather, Lorenz, a meteorologist with the Army
Air Corp in WWII, and later a professor of meteorology at MIT,
decided to simulate weather patterns by entering a simple system

of equations into what today would be considered a primitive but nevertheless capable computer.

Employing an algorithm that included fifteen variables like air pressure, wind speed, and air temperature, he ran the numbers to simulate a weather pattern. Based on the simulation printed out by the computer, a definite weather pattern emerged. Lorenz concluded that with the right data, it would be possible to accurately forecast weather on a consistent basis.

To confirm his research, Lorenz decided to run the model again. To save time, he began the simulation in the middle of the course by entering data that corresponded to the conditions he had entered in the original model. Since the data was almost the same as the original program with only a slight change, he expected the simulation of the weather generated by the computer would turn out the same.

To his complete surprise, however, the weather simulation the computer generated was completely different. It was puzzling. How could a miniscule change in the data he originally entered in the computer produce such a dramatic change in the simulated forecast?

After eliminating computer error, he realized the culprit was a rounded decimal number in the computer printout. While the computer worked with six-digit precision, the printout function rounded variables off to a three-digit number. So a value of 0.506127 printed as 0.506, a difference so small that it should not have made a difference.[9]

Eventually, Lorenz concluded that the things that change the world are not big things after all but little, seemingly inconsequential things. Today his theory has been generally accepted by the scientific community; hence, we have the origin of the butterfly effect or chaos theory.

Hurricane formation is much more complicated of course than a tiny butterfly that disturbs the atmosphere leading to a tropical depression. They are typically birthed off the west coast of Africa or

---

[9] Gleick, *Chaos: Making a New Science*, 18.

east coast of South America when summer ocean temperatures are hot and the atmospheric conditions favorable. This usually occurs from late August through September.

Meteorologists using satellites and computer-generated models can see their formation taking place and, based on satellite data and upper atmospheric conditions, can predict with some degree of accuracy their likely formation and path, although this varies with the different models used in forecasting likely paths of the storm. However, even with all the technology, much of hurricane formation is still guesswork.

I watched for more than a week in advance the formation of Hurricane Idalia while it was still a tiny tropical depression spinning aimlessly between the Yucatan Peninsula of Mexico and the island of Cuba. What began as a minor depression meandering about eventually morphed into a category 4 hurricane once it crossed over the warm waters of the gulf. The damage it did to homes and property was horrific.

As a frequent visitor to Florida and with many friends who live there, I am conscious that it is not just the weather that is unpredictable. It is many other things as well.

34

Chaos in Creation

Chaos is the science of surprises, of the
non-linear and the unpredictable ... chaos
theory deals with things that are impossible
to predict like turbulence, weather, the
stock market our brain states and so on.
—James Gleick, *Chaos*

You and I live in the post-Flood age, an era when many other things in nature are difficult to accurately forecast. For example, we can, based on previous history, know an earthquake is likely to occur. However, we cannot predict with certainty when it will happen. These natural world events, nonlinear and unpredictable, are examples of chaos theory.

This evidence for chaos in nature has never been more evident than the way deadly viruses and bacteria spread. The recent COVID-19 virus is a perfect example. When a single human was infected by the tiny virus under development in a lab in Wuhan, China, he left work apparently unaware he was sick. As we know, the virus quickly spread throughout the world, resulting in the deaths of millions of people and the disruption of economies. You may have been infected as well.

The bubonic plague, possibly the most infamous of bacterial diseases in the history of our world, had its origins along a trade route somewhere in Asia around 1347. It is theorized a tiny bacterium jumped into the flea population and from a single flea to the rodent population. During this time, it went from what was innocuous to a virulent form.

The tiny bacterium, likely spread by a tiny flea, eventually infected men guiding the caravans of trade goods from the Gobi Desert of China to the Ukrainian port city of Caffa. There the men of the caravan offloaded the trade goods onto Italian ships. The horrific disease, initially carried by rodents and fleas and now infecting the caravan traders spread quickly among the sailors on the cargo ships bound for Messina, Italy.

By the time the sailors arrived at their destination, most of the crew on the vessels were dead or dying.

Family and friends, upon learning of the sick sailors, rushed to the harbor to claim the bodies of their loved ones or to minister to the sick.

When the plague first broke out, people were ignorant of the most basic practices of cleanliness, enabling the bacterium in its airborne state to spread rapidly throughout the general population.

Eventually known as the "black death" because of its effect on the body (swollen nymph nodes), the plague quickly spread throughout Europe, eventually killing as many as 22 million people, a third of the population.

Stories of panic, difficulty in disposing of bodies, and the overall impact of the disease are well documented, including its impact on European confidence in the church. Why the church? Barbara Tuchman, in her classic discussion of the medieval world, concluded, "To the people at large there could be but one explanation—the wrath of God."[10]

Many people in our day tend to believe the same thing—that bad things happen to bad people. They are also puzzled when tragedy intrudes upon the righteous. In Luke 13, Jesus put an end to speculations like this when he discussed the tragic deaths of certain

---

[10] Tuchman, Barbara W. *A Distant Mirror*, 107, Alfred A. Knopf, Inc., 1978.

Galileans at the hands of Pilate and a similar tragedy that occurred when workers on the Tower of Siloam were killed as the result of an apparent structural failure.

Were these victims of tragedy worse sinners than all others? In Luke 13:3, Jesus said, "I tell you, no! But unless you repent, you too will all perish."

The truth Jesus was illustrating is that in a fallen world subject to unpredictability and chaos, the evil acts of bad people and random structural failures can occur at any time and place, impacting not only those who do not trust in Jesus but Christians as well.

The lesson is clear; whenever and wherever things go wrong in a fallen world, as they will, we need to be prepared to meet our Creator because we do not know when our life in this world will come to an end or the circumstances that could lead to it.

I know this in part because my people experienced something like the bubonic plague, although on a much smaller scale. What led to this was an economic opportunity.

In the spring of 1853, two members of my tribe, intent on securing a deal for oil rendered from whales they had harvested, made the journey thousands of miles south along the coast from our small village to the city of San Francisco, then headquarters for the whaling industry.

Unlike other tribes along the coast, my people had a long history of hunting whales for their food value. But now that they had encountered Europeans, they realized that they could purchase modern goods like guns, pots, pans, knives, and axes with the profits gained from rendering oil from the whales they hunted.

Whale oil in the 1850s was critical to the early development of America and was in high demand as a source for perfumes, lighting city lamps, as well as providing lubrication for the machinery of America's rapidly growing industry.

The two tribal members, having surveyed the possibilities for economic development, returned home aboard a small sailing ship known as a brig.

Unknown to them, also on the ship was a man who had recently contracted smallpox while in San Francisco. Through the years, San Francisco had become known for having serious outbreaks of the virus.

Originating in Europe, the smallpox virus was originally spread to the Americas by the Spanish during the Discovery Era.

Naturally the indigenous populations in both South America and North America, lacking immunity from the deadly disease, died in the hundreds of thousands and even millions, which made them more susceptible to being conquered by the Spanish conquistadors. In the case of my tribe, the Makah men on the brig began feeling the onset of the disease.

According to a trader, Samuel Hancock who lived among the Makah at the time, once the two men reached shore, they were already desperately ill. One of the men died shortly thereafter, while the other recovered. However, the deadly disease soon spread throughout the community.

Hancock wrote a brief report on what he had witnessed. "The dead were so numerous I could scarcely walk round my house and was obliged to have holes dug where I deposited fifteen or twenty bodies in each."[11]

Understandably, people panicked as family and friends began getting sick and dying. To escape the deadly virus, many fled across the Strait of Juan de Fuca to the Native village of Nit Nat on Vancouver Island.

This spread the disease to the people living there and eventually to other Native communities.

Today there are unmarked mass graves in various places in my community, a testimony to the way a microscopic virus can mutate into deadly carnage affecting thousands.

Why would our Creator allow chaos and unpredictability to be the reality of the Third Era of Mother Earth?

---

[11] Hancock, Samuel, *Letter Regarding Smallpox Epidemic at Neah Bay*, 1855.

Part of the answer is this: Humankind, after the first two eras of Mother Earth and despite all God had done for them, had demonstrated a willingness to rebel against the Creator, forget His gracious providence, and resort to the worship of false gods. In Jeremiah 17:9, we read why we are prone to rebellion against our Creator. "The heart is deceitful above all things and beyond cure. Who can understand it?"

To ensure we would be reminded of our need to depend upon Him, the post-Flood world appears to have become more chaotic and unpredictable than the previous world, serving in all its manifestation as a daily reminder proclaiming the glory of God while also warning us that we need to trust Him in all our circumstances.

To borrow from C. S. Lewis's discussion on the pain and suffering that characterize our individual lives, the various manifestations of nature in its beauty and beast character "whispers to us in our pleasures, speaks (to us) in our conscience but shouts in our pains."[12]

Following the Great Flood of Noah's time, a new generation of people began to repopulate Mother Earth. These were our ancestors. Thus began the Third Era of Mother Earth. But in less than three hundred years, people began to forget our Creator God and began to worship idols of wood and stone and, as is the pattern accompanying idolatry, resorted to child sacrifice.

---

[12] Lewis, C. S. *The Problem of Pain*, Harper One, 2015.

35

The Tower of Babel

FOLLOWING THE GREAT FLOOD OF NOAH'S TIME, MOTHER EARTH began to recover from the massive traumas it had endured, and birds, animals, and people began to reproduce and multiply in accord with our Creator's purpose to restart His creation.

And while the single landmass of the pre-Flood era could have split into the seven continents during the traumas associated with the Great Flood, an assumption many credible theologians believe occurred, I theorize the single landmass remained intact, albeit vastly changed.

One obvious difference in this new earth was that it appears the atmosphere surrounding it was different, allowing for the deadly rays that regularly enter earth's atmosphere that contribute to the aging process. Evidence for this is that people did not live as long after the Great Flood. And for the first time, people and animals began to eat meat.

One thing did not change, however. Post-Flood people who should have known better, the descendants of Noah's children, began to turn away from the Creator and worship idols.

One of the leaders of this rebellion was a man named Nimrod, a person of evident stature and charismatic personality. He also had a serious character flaw. He did not honor God, and some commentators credit him with introducing idolatry into the post-Flood world.

Born some three hundred years after his great-grandfather Noah, Nimrod is thought to have been angry with God for destroying the previous world with floodwaters. Appropriate to his rebellious nature, his name literally meant "We will rebel."

Evidently of impressive leadership skills, Nimrod soon rose to prominence. In Genesis 10:8, it is said that he "became a mighty warrior on the earth."

It seems like a compliment, but hidden behind his impressive credentials was his dark and rebellious nature.

Jewish historian Josephus credits him with inspiring the building of the Tower of Babel, a symbol of pride and defiance.[13]

In Genesis 11:4, we get a glimpse of his defiant nature. "Come, let us build ourselves a city, with a tower that reaches to the heavens, so that we may make a name for ourselves; otherwise, we will be scattered over the face of the whole earth."

The construction of the great ziggurat, as these early towers of that era were known, introduces us to the beginning of cities and architectural innovation that in this instance was intended to defy God's command that people spread out across the entire earth. The Tower of Babel was in that sense built in defiance of God's command, a rallying point intended to encourage people to stay near one another.

Our Creator saw all this unfolding of course and responded, "If as one people speaking the same language, they have begun to do this, then nothing they plan to do will be impossible for them" (Genesis 11:6).

This was no small admission on the part of God. It encapsulates this warning: behind humankind's genius for invention lurks the potential for turning what seems good into a means of defiance of God.

The Tower of Babel and newly developing cities were not only symbolic of humankind's genius and technological skills but also a declaration of independence from God.

A mentor of mine, a Christian psychiatrist, reminded me that technology, "like gasoline thrown on a fire, serves as an accelerant to human sin."

---

[13] Whiston, William. *The Life and Works of Flavius Josephus*, 39. Philadelphia: John C. Winston Company.

I have previously cited the invention of the clock and how the mechanics that went into its development spun off many other innovations in industry, eventually serving as a catalyst for change throughout the world. Most people would say this was all good.

However, we have also seen the dark side of innovation. We need only consider the internet, which is so beneficial in enhancing communication while providing a platform for theft of someone's identity, spreading lies, and serving as a means of polluting morals as well as radically shaping political convictions. Its ability to shape people's beliefs explains in part why our culture has gone through rapid change in a short period of time.

And now we are facing the introduction of artificial intelligence (AI). AI was designed with competitive intelligence far exceeding the human capacity to store and process information. It can outthink you.

And it can be programmed to access information on almost any subject far exceeding human capabilities. If you have the app, you can ask an AI chat box any question on any subject, including religion and politics, and it will give you answers that are not necessarily true but also seem to be convincing. This innovation is gathering a lot of followers.

As an example, an AI chat box was opened in early January 2023, and within a short period of time, it is estimated that it had over 100 million active users, the fastest-growing consumer application in history.

And this is why some people consider artificial intelligence the greatest danger to humankind: it can be programmed to make decisions independent of human controls. No less a brilliant mind than Elon Musk has warned that the increasing proliferation of AI without constraints poses the greatest threat to our society.

Imagine that kind of intelligence in a robot, your car, your cell phone, or any other form of communication, including weapons of war.

Already we have learned what Eric Snowden, a former computer consultant now in exile, revealed concerning US intelligence agency's ability to utilize technology to monitor our phone calls and emails—all under the guise of national security.

This capability will only be multiplied if AI is applied to achieve similar kinds of intrusions into our lives. And then of course thieves will be able to access information on a scale unprecedented once they devise their own applications for AI. Recently, it has been incorporated into the IRS as a means of uncovering tax cheaters.

Already weapons manufacturers in countries throughout the world are devising AI applications for aircraft, missiles, and a host of other weapons of war. What will prevent nations from using it to accelerate the spread of weapons of mass destruction and virus development as weapons of terror?

What can be learned from revisiting Babylon and the Tower of Babel, and the man known as Nimrod, is that from the beginning there has been an evil world system working behind the scenes of history that is opposed to all that is of God. And behind the spirit of innovation and rebellion is the spirit of Nimrod, the "We will rebel" spirit that uses innovation to accomplish evil.

To prevent the too soon introduction of technology that could thwart God's intent to scatter His people throughout the earth and to disrupt His plan of salvation, God did something amazing. He confused the languages and scattered the people across the world.

In doing so, He preserved nations and tribes from being absorbed into a powerful system that was already advancing quickly toward the evil culture that led to the destruction of the previous world.

By confusing the languages of the nations and tribes at Babel, He not only slowed technological innovation but also preserved the diversity of people He created, thus setting the stage for the Gospel of Jesus to spread to the entire world.

Always and forever, God reigns supreme over the evil designs of sinful humankind. Proverbs 19:21 assures us, "Many are the plans in a person's heart, but it is the Lord's purpose that prevails."

36

The Earth Divided

Two sons were born to Eber: One was named
Peleg, because in his time the earth was divided.
—Genesis 10:25

ACCORDING TO GENESIS, PRIOR TO THE GREAT FLOOD, THE
habitable land was composed of a single landmass. Europe, Asia,
Africa, Antarctica, Australia, New Zealand, North America, and
South America were a part of a supercontinent surrounded by a vast
body of water.

Naturally, through the years, skeptics of biblical revelation have
questioned such an idea. However, not everyone.

One of the first scientists in modern times to propose the idea of
the existence of a supercontinent was a German meteorologist, Alfred
Wegener, who in 1915 theorized that the earth's six continents plus
Australia had once been part of a single landmass. He named this
supercontinent Pangaea, from the Greek word meaning "all one land."

He wasn't the first to consider this possibility. Britain's Francis
Bacon, a philosopher who lived in the mid-1500s, had proposed a
similar theory.

What initially caught Wegner's attention leading to his theory
was the way the continents appeared to fit together like pieces of a
giant puzzle. South America and Africa as well as North America
and Europe looked to have once been joined as one.

Eventually he noticed similarities in the distribution of like kinds of fossils throughout the world, including Antarctica.

He noted too that some birds and animals unique to the west coast of Africa exist in only one other place, the east coast of South America.

He also found evidence of similar geologic formations—rocks of the same age and type—that appeared to link the American Appalachians, the Atlas Mountains in Africa, and the mountains of the highlands of Scotland, a kind of common DNA.

And since he was a meteorologist, he noticed too that there appeared to be a time when a uniform, tropical climate existed throughout much of the earth.

Evidence of palm trees and other warm-weather flora have since been discovered deep below the ice sheets of Antarctica as well as throughout much of the rest of the world.

There seemed to be evidence too of similar pattern glacial scouring on rocks found in Africa, India, and South America, the matching indentations, or scratches, indicative that they may have been subject to stresses caused by the same ice sheet.

Nevertheless, for most of modern history, scientists remained skeptical of the existence of a single continent—until recently.

In 1959 marine geologists aboard the research vessel *Glomar Explorer* completed a study of a newly charted ridge of underwater mountains that winds unbroken for 12,000 miles along the floor of the Atlantic Ocean separating North America from Europe and Africa from South America.

Much to the scientist's surprise, it appeared that the underwater ridge came together with the European and North American landmasses like two pieces of a puzzle, just as did the South American and African landmasses. Antarctica was linked to India and India to the rest of Asia.

To the formerly skeptical scientists, this was evidence that there was a time in the geologic history of the earth when Pangaea separated into the seven continents we have today.

Nevertheless, true to their theory of millions and billions of years of evolution, scientists calculated that the separation of the continents likely occurred 170 to 200 million years ago.[14]

The biblical time line is vastly different. If we assume there was once a single landmass that the Creator in Peleg's time divided, this would have occurred some three hundred years after the Great Flood of Noah's time.

By then nations and tribes had already begun to differentiate and to repopulate the earth and people were forming into various tribes and nations.

And some, like the highly advanced Sumerians, were building large cities, developing new cultures, and establishing technologically superior civilizations that included a form of writing, innovations in structural design that led to the construction of the Tower of Babel, mathematics, astronomy, and production of goods.

While some biblical scholars suggest the reference to "the earth being divided" should not be taken literally but understood as a reference to the scattering of people across the face of the earth following the confusion of languages that followed the building of the Tower of Babel as described in Genesis 11:1, I propose the theory that this refers to an actual separation of the supercontinent and was intended to facilitate the dispersion of people.

In offering my theory, I am taking literally the statement "the earth was divided" to mean that our Creator separated what had been a single landmass, and in doing so, He suspended the laws governing the natural world so that the people and all the living creatures would not die in the process. I am of the faith that "for no word from God will ever fail" (Luke 1:37); thus, none of the laws regarding time and space and laws of motion or gravity supersede or limit His power and authority over all that He has created.

During this time, it is conceivable that He could have placed the people and animals in a deep sleep so that they would not experience

---

[14] *Life* magazine. "Jigsaw of the Primeval World," 161, January 1970.

the traumas associated with the process of separation—not unlike the deep sleep Adam experienced when God took Eve from his side.

It is likely some of my readers will disagree with my hypothesis. I contend, however, that there will come a time when we witness the suspension of all the natural laws of the earth and the whole of the universe when, as biblical prophecies foretell, the Creator will cause the entire creation to disappear in one great explosion and then be recreated.

The apostle Peter, describing this momentous event, wrote, "But the day of the Lord will come like a thief. The heavens will disappear with a roar; the elements will be destroyed by fire, and the earth and everything done in it will be laid bare" (2 Peter 3:10). From this will come a new heaven and new earth.

The transformation of Mother Earth along with the entire universe will not take billions of years of evolution but will occur in the blink of an eye. And our Creator God will preserve us through that change.

Dividing Pangaea into seven continents while preserving the lives of the people seems by comparison to the creation of a new universe and a new earth, a small miracle. Is there anything in Native tradition that might support such a theory?

A few years ago, I came across a book, *The Elder Brothers,* written by British author Alan Ereira. He wrote about the Kogi, an indigenous people who reside in the high Andes of Colombia, South America. This unusual tribal people believe themselves to be the guardians of Mother Earth.

In their tradition, the Kogi have retained a narrative that seems to validate the story of a single continent. According to their tradition, they once lived side by side with their White brothers. They refer to themselves as the Elder Brothers and White Europeans as their Younger Brothers.

37

The Elder Brothers

We are the Elders, we were the Elders of all,
with greater knowledge, spiritual and material.
—Alan Ereira, *The Elder Brothers*

NONE OF THE TRIBES OF WHICH I AM ACQUAINTED HAVE A STORY of migrating across a land bridge connecting Siberia to Alaska. That doesn't mean it didn't happen, but I have not heard of it.

Being oral-history people, an event of so great a magnitude would surely have been noted and passed from generation to generation. After all, an epic journey from Asia across a land bridge to Alaska, especially during the Ice Age, would surely have taken a heroic effort involving motive, strategic planning, logistics, skilled leadership, and a vast supply of food. Campsites that have been excavated through the years in the hope of identifying migration paths from Siberia to North America as theorized by most archaeologists appear to show the earliest sites are in the south and not, as one would expect, the north.

Despite varying creation narratives, most North American tribes have held to their traditional beliefs of having been created in America. And this in the face of a multitude of anthropologists, geneticists, and archaeologists who over many years have attempted to explain Native American origins by citing the latest DNA evidence, migration theories, certain elements of archaeological findings, or some combination of all the above.

Truth is Native American origins have always been a mystery enshrouded by the fog of competing theories.

You may remember one of the more bizarre: Native people were remnants of the so-called Lost Ten Tribes of the Northern Kingdom of Israel.

And so, ongoing questions have remained. When and how did the various indigenous peoples arrive in the Americas? Did they swim? Come by canoe? Walk the long journey from Asia to North America and then South America?

Not many years ago, English author Alan Ereira, under the auspices of the British Broadcasting Company, and at the invitation of members of a unique tribe known as the Kogi, journeyed to a remote Colombian Native community living in the high Andes. They had an important message to tell the world. One that in the context had similarities not so far removed from my theory concerning landmass separation in Peleg's time.

Conducting his research at a time when environmental concerns were just beginning to rise to the top of the political agenda, Alan Ereira made his journey through dangerous drug cartel country to the place where the Kogi lived in relative isolation from the rest of the world. His opening comment began,

> For four centuries these people, the last surviving high civilization of pre-conquest America, have watched in silence from their hidden world in the mountains of Columbia. They have kept their world alive and intact, and kept their distance. Now, in what they fear may be the closing days of life on earth, they have summoned us to listen.[15]

Residing along the east coast of Colombia during the time of the discoverers, the ancestors of the Kogi, the Elder Brothers as they refer

---

[15] Ereira, Alan. *The Elder Brothers*. New York: Random House, 1990, 1.

to themselves, were the first to greet Columbus when he and his men landed on the shores of their homeland.

It was not a good first meeting. Gold, silver, land claims, and enslavement were foremost on the minds of Columbus and his men.

Once the Kogi discerned their motives, they fled to the high Andes, where they have resided in relative isolation for the last four hundred years. From their place in the mountains twenty-six miles from the sea and reaching as high as 19,000 feet, they have been able to remain in isolation.

All seemed well until the latter part of the twentieth century, when they were able to observe that the flora and fauna on the mountainsides were gradually disappearing.

Something was wrong with the Mother, their term for the earth, and they knew what it was. Beginning with Columbus, the Europeans they refer to as their Younger Brothers had brought a lust for gold and silver, digging up Mother to find these precious metals as well as stealing from the Natives. This was not good. It meant the world was dying.

In their way of thinking, the entire world of people was suspended on the same rope, and if Younger Brother continued to rip out the heart of the Mother, the world was going to come to an end.

That is the reason they decided to break their silence and communicate to the modern world what their ancient knowledge had preserved.

What caught my interest, however, was not their environmental concerns, which naturally fed environmentalists fears, but how these unusual people had preserved a narrative with similarities to the biblical story of the separation of the continents. The Elder Brothers, according to their tradition, believe they once shared the same geographical region as their European Younger Brothers. They further contended that Serankua, their name for the Creator, had gifted them with knowledge both "spiritual and material," while Younger Brother was given the gift of technology. But something was wrong. The Elder Brothers discerned Younger Brother did not understand how to wisely use his gift of technology; he lacked wisdom and understanding. This was dangerous. Serankua the Creator saw this too and discerned that the misuse of technology was going to adversely impact His creation. He determined to separate the brothers by creating a division in the land. He said, "Let us send them away to the other side and so that they shall not pass. I make a division—the sea."[16]

This reminded me of Genesis 11:6 when God the Father, God the Son, and God the Holy Spirit determined the hidden purpose for the building of Tower of Babel. "The Lord said, 'If as one people speaking the same language, they have begun to do this, then nothing they plan to do will be impossible for them.'" And just as in the Kogi narrative, our Creator not only confused the language, but He also separated the people into tribes and nations by causing them to disperse across the whole of the earth now divided into continents.

You can imagine the great consternation felt by the Kogi when the great sea that divided the brothers was crossed by Younger Brother. Seeing the damage that the delicate flora and fauna on the sides of the high Andes were experiencing due to industrial pollution was alarming.

Therein lies the substance of what are two very different points of view regarding Mother Earth and how we manage it.

The Elder Brothers sought to live in harmony with creation and not subdue it, while Younger Brother was determined to subdue and exploit its resources.

What their story illustrates is that there is a balance to be maintained in the relationship between Younger Brother and Elder Brother. We need the benefits of innovation and the technology of Younger Brother, and we need the resources Mother Earth provides while recognizing and preserving its delicate balance. But we also need the wisdom of those who correctly read the message Mother Earth is increasingly proclaiming to us. The Elder Brothers understood her

---

[16] Ibid., 74.

message. Younger Brother, on the other hand, continues to pursue innovations that if misused will lead to the destruction of the world. Underlying this is an even greater God purpose. Everything in our shared history is meant to teach us how to live as brothers and sisters and to find and experience God's redemptive purpose. As Acts 17:27 tells us, "He is not far from any one of us."

And the message Younger Brother and Elder Brother need to hear is that before time as we now experience it, God had determined to send His Son Jesus to rescue us from the consequences of the Fall and Mother Earth from the curse that has left it groaning and in travail while awaiting Jesus's return.

Just as in "the fullness of time, God sent His Son" to fulfill His promise made to Adam and Eve to redeem humankind, so too He has caused us, the brothers, to come together in this time and place.

And while people throughout the world have lost much of their original knowledge of the Creator, He has not left people of every nation and every tribe without the witness of who He is through the things He has created and the stories they tell.

The Elder Brothers had preserved a key element of God's purpose in causing people to disperse throughout the world. They understood too that creation has a message for us. It is anxiously calling us back to our Creator, to acknowledge His glory and to be thankful for all He has done for us.

38

Thunderbird and the Whale

> There was the Thunderbird, so huge it darkened the
> sky. He made the thunder sound with the beat of his
> wings. His eyes were flashing lightning. Then he flew
> straight down. But as he was about to hit the water,
> he swooped back up carrying a whale in his talons.
> —Makah elder

ONE OF THE MORE COMPELLING ASPECTS OF MY PEOPLE'S WAY OF LIFE is that they were hunters of the whale. I do not know of any other tribes on the West Coast that carried out this tradition. Nor do I know for how long my ancestors practiced this dangerous endeavor. I do know, however, that the government prohibited them from continuing to do so at the beginning of the twentieth century due to the diminishing numbers of whales caused by over harvesting by the large whaling fleet that had moved from the Atlantic Coast to the Pacific Coast.

Now that whales have recovered in sufficient numbers, my tribe has been trying to regain federal government approval to continue this ancient tradition. Unfortunately, there are many people who oppose them. Organizations like Greenpeace and other save-the-whale groups have opposed the tribe in federal court to prevent them from resuming their whaling tradition.

Typically, whale hunting was carried out in the spring of the year when gray whales and humpback whales were migrating off the coast. My tribe never took more than a few each year as needed.

Carefully selected men of the tribe would set out in forty-foot, cedar, dugout canoes with a crew of seven or eight men armed with harpoon, float bags made of sealskins, rope, and a single-minded determination to find their prey and then, with practiced stealth, come alongside an unsuspecting giant mammal and thrust a harpoon into its side.

That's when the adventure would become interesting. The giant animal weighing fifty tons or more, and with a harpoon in its side, would in a desperate effort to escape pull the canoe with rope and float bags attached on what had to be a terrifying ride through the sea. The crew could only hang on.

And then as they knew would happen, the giant beast of the sea would eventually tire, allowing the canoe to come along side one more time, thus affording a crew member time to strike a final death blow from a second harpoon that would end the pursuit and the life of the great whale.

Shortly afterward, a crewman trained to do so would dive into the cold Pacific waters and, with giant needle and sinew attached, sew the mouth of the whale shut so that it would not fill with water and sink to the bottom of the ocean.

Then with whale now in tow, the crew would pull it back to the village, where a great crowd would have assembled to greet them. Whale meat is highly nutritious and a great source of protein. As you might imagine, the crew pulling the giant whale to shore was honored for their prowess. Once on shore, the whale was divided and given to the chief, the whalers, and then to the rest of the community.

No part of the whale was wasted. Parts of the rib cage could be used to make hooks, wool beaters, combs, and various other useful items; the larger bones could be placed alongside the longhouses to redirect water away from the cedar structures.

As important as the whale was for food and necessary utilitarian items, perhaps much more important was its spiritual significance. In the minds of the Makah, there was a mystical, religious connection between the people and the Creator who they believed had miraculously provided the whale for the well-being of the people.

According to a narrative long accepted as a key element of my tribe's lore, at one point in their past, they were facing imminent starvation apparently due to a cataclysmic event that took place so far back in time no one could remember when or exactly what led to it. According to this ancient legend, the people were facing imminent starvation in a place where, as I have previously related, food sources of all kinds were almost always plentiful and easy to acquire.

Because I knew this, I always wondered what could possibly have been the reason for their desperate circumstances. Were the jagged rock formations along the coast a clue to whatever threatened my people? Could it have been a massive earthquake, something the area is known to have experienced? Did the Creator allow drought, earthquake, and tsunamis to call them to reverence and thankfulness? A giant tsunami seemed a possibility.

When I was a child, certain elders in our community related the story of a large seismic event accompanied by a massive wave that swept across our land from the ocean side to the Strait of Juan de Fuca, some five miles.

Based on the records kept by the Japanese who experienced a tsunami from that same event, it is believed that it had occurred in AD 1700. Could that tsunami be an explanation for the desperate state of my people?

One reason this is a possibility is that not more than a hundred miles off the coast is a major fault. Not much farther out to sea is an undersea volcano, the Cobb Sea Mount. Clearly the land and adjacent sea near where my people live have had a volatile history.

And so, it is possible a large earthquake could have been the origin of the story of Thunderbird and Whale. However, I theorize it might well have been the result of something even greater, very possibly the continental shift I discussed earlier.

According to my theory, God would have preserved animals and people during the shift. At the same time, the disruption accompanying such a massive event may have meant the survival of the tribe could have reached a critical state. If that were the case and all seemed lost, I believe God our Creator would have intervened to ensure their survival by providing them with a whale delivered in a miraculous manner. One that involved a giant bird clutching in its talons a great whale, accompanied by thunder and lightning serpents.

According to Makah legend, Thunderbird, a mythical bird of gigantic size clutching a whale in its talons and with lightning serpents surrounding it, flew down to the village and deposited the whale amid the people, thus saving them from starvation.

So deeply entrenched has this story of deliverance been in my tribe's tradition that it has survived thousands of years of oral history. And throughout the annals of time, the elders of my tribe have attached a deeply spiritual significance to the story of Thunderbird and Whale. This is revealed in the preparation for the hunt.

Prior to the hunt, months of training were required. This included not only physical training to build strength and stamina but spiritual training as well. Months in advance of the hunt, men carefully chosen for this purpose would rise early in the morning and bathe themselves in the cold streams that flowed through the village. It is said they would also toughen themselves by rubbing nettles on their bodies, all the while singing songs and saying prayers on behalf of the whale that it would not suffer.

For them, Thunderbird and Whale were evidence of a miraculous deliverance from extinction, its symbolism in tribal art preserving the memory of this miraculous event much in the way the cross signifies the same for millions of Christians. And ever after, the people believed that the whale they hunted for food was giving its life for the good of the people.

For generations this narrative has continued to live on in the art and story of my people. A tribal artist was eventually commissioned to create an official tribal emblem based on this legendary event.

To this day, Thunderbird clutching a whale in its talons, surrounded by lightning serpents—symbols of great power, wisdom, and glory—represent the official logo of the tribe.

With a long history of whaling, the massive animal wasn't just a food source. It had a spiritual component; it reminded the people of the Creator's grace in delivering them from certain calamity.

Furthermore, it was a reminder that creation is often subject to unpredictable behaviors that can jeopardize our well-being. And further that our Creator God alone can provide for our needs when creation, subject to chaos, unleashes the storms of life.

However the story originated, its message is clear. When nature is most threatening and our survival is in doubt, our Creator can and will come to our aid. We just need to set aside our pride, repent, and trust in Him.

39

Native American Prophets

We were told we would see America come and go.
And in a sense America is dying from within because
it is without instructions on how to live on earth.
Everything is coming to a time where prophecy
and man's inability to live on earth in a spiritual
way will come to a crossroad of great problems.
—Floyd Red Crow Westerman, Hopi Tribe

FOLLOWING WORLD WAR II, AMERICA EMERGED AS THE LEADER OF the free world, a dominant economic and military power that other nations wanted to emulate. We were in a sense the big dog on the planet. And with the end of the world war and the formation of the United Nations, it seemed sanity among the nations of the earth would finally prevail. Nations could now solve disputes in a rational way and peace would result throughout the world. Or so people thought.

Sadly human greed, bitter memories of ancient feuds—think Russia and Ukraine—the lust for power, and other aspects of human sin reveal how futile world peace is. Wars continue to plague humankind at an alarming rate despite the UN. You need only to think of Israel and Hamas and how since the famous Oslo Accords of 1993 calling for Palestinian self-rule and Jewish security peace efforts have fallen apart.

Nevertheless, in the positive outlook following the postwar era, optimism seemed to prevail. Fueled by growing industry and high demand for American goods, our economy began to flourish, and people were optimistic that the economy was only going to get better and better, a view especially held by the baby boomers (the children born just after the war). For these children, the American dream of owning an affordable home and a new car was expected; jobs were plentiful, pay was good, and every indicator was that you could achieve whatever you wanted if you put forth the effort. North Americans exemplified what Canadian author Douglas John Hall described as "the officially Optimistic Society."[17]

Of course, that wasn't true for all Americans, especially not the original inhabitants of this land who had been removed from their traditional homelands and forced to live on resource-poor, isolated reservation land while being made subject to a socialistic form of governance that hindered their ability to achieve self-determination and guaranteed they would always be poverty-stricken.

Going back in time before the coming of "Younger Brother" to the Americas, many Native American tribal prophets anticipated the coming of Europeans and the empire that would eventually emerge, and they would suffer as a result. But they also seem to have known that the American empire would eventually come to an end.

Did the Creator appear before them and tell them this so that they would be prepared? Especially since the newcomers to the land would bring a diametrically different philosophy regarding time, the stewardship of the earth and its resources.

Naturally you would think that Native Americans, long associated with the careful management of all things created, would in this present age of the Green New Deal thinkers and global warming advocates join in the chorus of those who place the blame for global warming on industry, fossil fuels, and careless manipulators of natural world resources. Much of their focus is on America and

---

[17] Hall, Douglas John. *Lighten Our Darkness.* Philadelphia: The Westminster Press, 1976, 36.

almost none on the biggest contributors to atmospheric pollution today: China and India.

While humans have certainly contributed much to the problems facing the environment, my contention has been that the core reason for huge problems like global warming and a host of other potential natural disasters is the curse that resulted from the Fall.

Our failure to honor our Creator and our willingness to defy His righteous laws are at the heart of the natural world's sometimes aberrant behaviors. And for that reason, we can never expect to save the earth from eventual disasters until we first reconcile with Him. And that must begin with repentance.

One tribe that has preserved a unique perspective on this is a people I have not personally had much contact with except to drive near their homeland some years ago. They are the Hopi people of Oraibi, Arizona.

Hopi elders have long had a tradition of visions and prophecies. They were afforded an opportunity to appear before the United Nations General Assembly on December 10, 1992, where they shared a message that must have fascinated if not stunned the world's leaders of that time.

According to Hopi tradition, they originally came from the underworld. Once they made it to the earth's surface, a woman they refer to as "Spiderwoman" was said to have met them and then given them instructions on how to live on the earth in a way that would preserve it and honor the Creator. They made a pledge to live simply and adhere to the Creator's instructions. However, it was made clear to them that if they did not do so, things would go badly. So badly the Creator would have to return to straighten out the mess.

Speaking before UN members representing the nations of the world, the Hopi spokesmen Thomas Banyacya and Martin Gashwesoma offered a history of the world that surely must have surprised them. They spoke of a time when all the people of the world spoke the same language. But people became selfish, power hungry, and turned away from the Creator's spiritual laws. This resulted in a worldwide flood accompanied with earthquakes. A few survived and came to a second world. However, repeating the mistakes of the first world led to the destruction of that world too, this time caused by the Ice Age.

Communicating in their traditional language translated by interpreters, the Hopi elders then spoke of the increasing number of earthquakes, horrific storms, and other aberrant manifestations of Mother Nature taking place today. These, they maintained, were the result of the same disregard for the Creator and His spiritual and moral laws that had led to the demise of previous worlds.

Unless there was a turning back to Him and a renewed willingness to follow His spiritual laws, nature would bring worse disasters upon humankind. This was a message the world leaders needed to hear.

As a Native American Christian with a longtime interest in certain aspects of natural world behaviors, I am convinced there is much truth to what these spokespeople from the Hopi tribe had to say. We are in trouble as a nation and so too our world because we no longer honor the Creator or His spiritual laws.

Although the Hopi delegation to the UN did not specify what spiritual laws were being violated, they hinted at the gross immorality and lust for power and greed evident in our present age. They noted that women dressing like men and men exposing themselves in nakedness were evidence of this change in morality. They could have found support for their message concerning immorality and its consequences in Paul's catalogue of sins listed in Romans 1.

One thing seems particularly ironic in the message coming from a people long marginalized. God is affording America and the nations of the world a unique opportunity to hear warnings from a people we might not expect: a remote tribe living on the edge of a desert region in Arizona and New Mexico.

40

The Fifth Era of Mother Earth

If my people, who are called by my name,
will humble themselves and pray and seek
my face and turn from their wicked ways,
then I will hear from heaven, and I will
forgive their sin and will heal their land.
—2 Chronicles 7:14

NATIVE AMERICAN PROPHETS, AS IN THE CASE OF THE HOPI elders, have long been speaking out regarding their concerns for America. They are not alone.

The scientific community too, including the geologists, seismologists, astrophysicists, biologists, and other science disciplines, are reading the signs in the heavens above as well as here on the earth below and are seeing potential for natural catastrophes across our country and the world due to a variety of causes.

Among some of their concerns are rising ocean levels due to ice melting in Greenland and Antarctica, the potential for asteroids hitting the earth with devastating consequences, and massive amounts of radiation from an exploding star. During the summer of 2023, much of America experienced the hottest temperatures in recorded history. This resulted in violent storms, flooding, forest fires, tornadoes, and hurricanes.

Even as I write this, the hurricane I referenced earlier is forming between the Yucatan Peninsula of Mexico and the island of Cuba and is beginning to strengthen as it moves slowly northward over the hot waters of the Gulf Coast of Florida. When it reaches land, it will cause significant damage to coastal homes and businesses.

It is not just Florida that experiences life-threatening situations. They exist wherever people live. One of the more dangerous is the West Coast where, as I related, earthquakes and volcanoes are a constant threat.

As you may know, seismologists have long been warning that the San Andreas Fault, which runs north from the Salton Sea in Southern California along a line through Los Angeles to San Francisco and beyond, is by all estimates poised to erupt at any time. As sophisticated as our modern technology has become, it is not possible to predict exactly when the fault will suddenly release the stress building up through the years, resulting in what is expected to be a powerful earthquake.

Imagine the horrific consequences for the state of California when it finally erupts. Buildings will collapse, roadways will buckle, bridges will fall, and countless lives will be lost or injured.

Near my childhood home, another major fault even more dangerous than the San Andreas fault lies just off the coast stretching from Northern California to British Columbia. Known as the Cascadia Subduction Zone, the Juan de Fuca plate is sliding underneath (subducting) the continental US plate. At some point, the pressure will be too great, resulting in a massive earthquake and tsunami. This is the same fault that caused the massive tsunami that impacted my people in AD 1700. Now just three hundred years later, it is locked and loaded and ready to go off again.

When the resulting stresses finally reach their tipping point, seismologists have predicted that an earthquake of nine or higher on the seismographic scale will likely occur. The resulting tsunami could potentially inundate coastal towns from Northern California to Washington State and the quake itself would do inestimable damage in major cities like Seattle and Portland. Some estimates suggest that as many as 16,000 people between Oregon and Washington State would be killed. Countless others would be injured, lose their homes to damage, and much of the infrastructure, such as bridges, large buildings, and highways, would be destroyed.

An event of this magnitude would comprise one of the greatest natural disasters in the history of America—unless you consider what would happen if Yellowstone were suddenly to become active.

Yellowstone is often referred to as a "super volcano." Encompassing 2.2 million acres, America's first national park is one of the largest volcanoes in the world and one of the most dangerous. With over 10,000 hypothermals and five hundred active geysers, it is beginning to show signs that are cause for concern. While the United States Geologic Survey monitors Yellowstone for signs of possible eruption and has assured the public that everything is OK, there are signs that suggest magma below the surface is moving. Park officials continue to assure the public that an eruption is not imminent, even though they have had to close some areas of the park to visitors because of new geyser activity. There has also been an increase in unusual animal behavior. Do they sense something is occurring under the earth?

Were this megavolcano to erupt, the consequences for surrounding states and the whole of America, even the world, would be a disaster exceeding anything we have experienced. Neighboring states like Idaho, Wyoming, Montana, the Dakotas, and states farther east would be inundated by ash so thick it would blot out the sun, bury crops under ash, and turn day into night across much of the United States.

All these potential natural catastrophes, and many other signs in the sun, the moon, and the stars and the politics of nations at odds with each other, are clear signs pointing to the soon return of Jesus. Depending on your faith, these potential disasters may be disturbing, so much so that you may not want to think about them; but if so, you will miss one of the most important messages Mother Earth is trying to communicate in all its dire expressions: this earth is not our final home; heaven is. And as I related earlier in my book, Mother Earth is pregnant and this is her third trimester. She is experiencing much distress. During her birth pangs, she can't wait for the birth of the new heavens and earth. She can't wait for Jesus to return to set everything straight.

Seeing the suffering of innocent people caught up in war zones or death and destruction resulting from a natural catastrophe of one sort or another makes me anxious too for Jesus to return.

Therefore, what you see in nature, however it may at times reflect beauty, is but a foreshadowing of far better things to come: the Fifth and Final Era of Mother Earth. The return of paradise lost. That is what her birth pangs are trying to communicate to us.

Here are some of the things I most look forward to when our Creator restores paradise: Whatever is beautiful about this present earth will pale by comparison to what our Creator God is preparing for His children in the eternity to come. And even more wonderful, in the new world to come, we will experience joy, love, and peace in the presence of our family members and our brothers and sisters in Christ from all nations and tribes who have been enabled by the Holy Spirit working in their lives to overcome the evils of this present age. And of course, we will no longer experience the curse of sin. I take that to mean no more sickness, no more war, no more aging, no more physical or mental deficiencies, no more prejudice and injustice, and no more will our children experience calamity. And in the presence of Jesus, we will be surrounded by love. Love for Him and love for all people saved by the blood of the Lamb, Jesus Christ.

The apostle Paul, who was given a vision of this coming reality, said this: "What no eye has seen, what no ear has heard, and what no human mind has conceived the things God has prepared for those who love him" (1 Corinthians 2:9).

And Jesus, after telling his disciples of his impending death assured them,

> Do not let your hearts be troubled. You believe in
> God; believe also in me. My Father's house has many

rooms; if that were not so, would I have told you that I am going there to prepare a place for you? And if I go and prepare a place for you, I will come back and take you to be with me that you also may be where I am. (John 14:1–3)

Jesus went on from this conversation to tell his disciples in verse 4 He was "the way and the truth and the life" and that no one could enter the presence of God except through a faith relationship with Him. It is critical that we have a saving relationship with Jesus as a condition of receiving eternal life.

For those who won't accept this or choose to ignore Jesus, a rude awakening will occur when He returns. Because they never trusted in Him throughout their lifetime and thought they were good enough on their own merits, they will miss out on an eternity with Jesus in the new heavens and new earth.

The devil knows his end is near and is doing all he can to prevent people from knowing Jesus. A liar, an imitator of light, and a deceiver of people, he wants to take as many people as possible with him to the hell God has prepared for him and his demon followers.

In a sense, the unfolding history of our world is comparable to a game of chess being played out in front of us, a contest between the Grand Master Jesus and Satan, his challenger.

As the game unfolds, everyone who knows the finer intricacies of the game can see that Jesus, the Grand Master, is far superior to his challenger in intellect and skill and that the game is over long before the clock runs out. It is just a matter of time before checkmate and the game ends. Jesus is the winner and is crowned champion.

Naturally, if you don't follow the game, none of this will make sense. In the same way, if you don't know God's Word, you won't understand how everything unfolding in the world is leading to the soon return of Jesus and His coronation as Lord of Lords and King of Kings.

In the real world, the contest between Jesus and Satan ended when, while hanging on the cross and breathing his last, Jesus proclaimed, "It is finished!" At that very moment, the hypothetical game of chess I described was over. On the cross, and while enduring God the Father's wrath, Jesus defeated sin, death, and the devil, and in doing so, He secured His children's eternal future.

As I have previously related, all of creation, including the whole of the vast universe, knows this too and is "groaning in travail" in anticipation of the day when Jesus returns and restores His chosen people, the entire universe, and Mother Earth to perfection.

But what about you? Are you a believer in Jesus who acknowledges you are a sinner and unworthy and unable by your own righteousness to merit eternal life? Sadly, some people I know think that because they are good people and live an exemplary life they will be allowed to enter heaven. Good enough on one's own merits, regardless of one's earthly achievements and the adoration that often accompanies worthwhile accomplishments, will not be enough to get one to heaven. Only a genuine repentance and faith in Jesus, who suffered and died on the cross for our sins, affords sinful humans the right to enter heaven.

Are you ready to meet Jesus when He returns? If not, I encourage you to prayerfully consider receiving Him as your Savior and Lord. You will be happy you did for all eternity. And that is a long time.

Bibliography

Adams, Douglas. *A Hitchhiker's Guide to the Galaxy*. Random House, 1980.

Boorstin, Daniel. *The Discoverers*. New York: Random House, 1985.

Epoch News, July 19–25, 2023.

Ereira, Alan. *The Elder Brothers*. New York: Random House, 1990.

Gleick, James. *Chaos: Making a New Science*. New York: Penguin Books, 1987.

Hall, Douglas John. *Lighten Our Darkness*. Philadelphia: The Westminster Press, 1976.

Hancock, Samuel. *Letter Regarding Smallpox Epidemic at Neah Bay*, 1855.

Jowell, Benjamin. *A Translation of Aristotle's Book One, Politics, Section V.*, 350 BC.

Lewis, C. S. *The Problem of Pain*. Harper One, 2015.

Life magazine. "Jigsaw of the Primeval World," January 1970.

Pieper, Francis. *Christian Dogmatics*. Concordia Publishing Co., 1957.

Tuchman, Barbara W. *A Distant Mirror*. Alfred A. Knopf, Inc., 1978.

Tyler, S. Lyman. *A History of Indian Policy*. US Bureau of Indian Affairs, 1973.

Vanity Fair, June 2008. Condensation of the Michael Dobs's book *One Minute to Midnight*.

Walsh, Michael. *The Devil's Pleasure Palace*. New York: Encounter Books, 2015.

Whiston, William. *The Life and Works of Flavius Josephus*. Philadelphia: John C. Winston Company.

About the Author

Rev. Dr. Don Johnson was raised on the Makah Indian reservation. After becoming a believer he felt the call to ministry. After graduating from college he returned to his hometown where for 20 years he served as a pastor and tribal leader. Following his service with his tribe he spent the next 20 years working with native peoples in North America developing Christian leadership skills. His perspective as a Native American affords a unique insight into the current issues facing America. He makes the argument that America must remain steadfast in holding to its foundation as a Christian nation.

Rev. Dr. Don Johnson resides in Hudson, Wisconsin and can be contacted via email at the following: domach321@gmail.com.

Printed in the United States
by Baker & Taylor Publisher Services